BLOODY

HISTORY

GLASGOW

BLOODY SCOTTISH HISTORY

GLASGOW

BRUCE DURIE

The History Press

For Jamie, who really likes the place!

'... an opera nobody performs nowadays, an opera called Scottish History.'
Janine, Alasdair Gray, 1982

'The trouble with Freud is that he never had to play the old Glasgow Empire
on a Saturday night after Rangers and Celtic had both lost.'
Ken Dodd

The History Press
The Mill, Brimscombe Port
Stroud, Gloucestershire, GL5 2QG
www.thehistorypress.co.uk

British Library Cataloguing in Publication Data.
A catalogue record for this book is available from the British Library.

ISBN 978 0 7524 8289 7

Typesetting and origination by The History Press
Printed in Great Britain

CONTENTS

ACKNOWLEDGEMENTS

THIS BOOK DEALS with the high and low notes of a truly great city. This Fifer was welcomed – and occasionally mocked in a friendly manner – by Glaswegians for several years before reverting to type and responding to what Kipling dubbed 'the call of the East' – but in this case only as far east as Kirkcaldy.

Sincere thanks (and a few apologies) are due to all those who watch while a book is written:

Frances Durie, who never does anything but encourage.

Jamie, Carolyn, Corinne, Natasha and Rowan, who treated all my rantings with amused tolerance.

The warm-hearted, funny, gregarious, knowledgeable, verbal and occasionally rubber Glaswegians.

And the inimitable Angel of the Red Pencil, Cate Ludlow at The History Press, who talked me into it.

PRE-HISTORY

A GREAT PLACE TO GO CANOEING

WALK AROUND GLASGOW with a geologist and you'll hear all about raised beaches and how the Clyde at what later became Glasgow was a few miles wide, covering much of what is now the city, as far as the Cathcart Hills. Yet it was inhabited, and provided a fine living.

How do we know? Because of the discovery of canoes and other artefacts around the Trongate and the Cross, covered by centuries of silt and gravel. One came to light in 1780 when St Enoch's church was being built, and another during the excavations for the Tontine buildings – plus a few more nearby, and later examples on the Southside. They were made by hollowing and burning out a single oak log, probably using the polished stone hatchet known as a 'celt', like the one found beside the Enoch's Square canoe, over 20ft down. So the Celts used celts. There is no question this implement was as handy for war as for DIY boat-building, a testament to the prevailing Glasgwegians' ability to use any tool for any purpose, regardless of what the label says.

So who were the prehistoric peoples, presumably living on the higher ground on the banks of the Molendinar River, where St Kentigern established his church and which later still bore the cathedral? Cathures (which, we are told, was the original name of what became *Glasgu*) must have been one of a series of river-bank settlements in the densely wooded Clyde Valley occupied by the people identified by the Roman geographer Ptolemy as the Damnonii, presumably Brythonic ('British') and speaking a language like Welsh, but quite possibly Picts or even Celts like their Gael cousins across in Ireland.

Today we tend to regard large stretches of water as barriers to travel, but they were the early equivalent of main roads. Recent archaeological evidence suggests the Gaels didn't so much arrive in Argyll and the west of Scotland in the fifth and sixth centuries as have constant interchange.

Canoes like these were unearthed at Springfield in 1847.

9

79-142 AD

CANNIBALS AND ROMANS

ONE THING YOU could say about the Romans is that they didn't mind a challenge. Julius Caesar invaded Britain in 55 BC and Claudius made other incursions a century later. But no one really bothered about the northern parts of Britannia until about AD 78, when Julius Agricola arrived to see what was up in the strath (valley) of the River Clyde and beyond. He bumped into what his son-in-law and chief PR man, Ptolemy, chose to call the Damnonii, who may have had their main settlement near the easily-defended hill later known as *Alt Clut* (the origin of 'Clyde'), and later still Dumbarton Rock, with its fortifications.

In the year AD 81, Agricola started the line of camps and fortifications between the Firths of Clyde and Forth but, to be honest, the Romans did not make much headway any further north. The famous battle of AD 88 at Mons Graupius (wherever that was, but possibly in the Grampians) is played up in Roman histories as a victory, but reading between the lines it's clear that they had a grudging respect for a territory and inhabitants they never really managed to subdue.

By the time the Antonine Wall was built, starting in AD 142, the fortification at present-day Old Kilpatrick was literally the end of the world – as far north-west as the Roman Empire ever got. Nor did they stay long, retreating to Hadrian's Wall and more or less the present Scottish-English border less than twenty years later.

The Romans had a few other away matches in AD 197, and the Emperor Septimius Severus decided to take his holidays in Scotland in AD 208, repairing some of the wall and securing the northern frontier to an extent, but even this re-occupation lasted only a few years. They eventually got fed up of the unruly locals, regular raids by land and sea from the next-door Picts, the Scotii from Dalriata in Ireland and a mysterious, supposedly cannibalistic lot called the Attacotti. St Jerome described an encounter with this fearsome tribe: 'In my youth I saw in Gaul the Attacotti, a British people, feeding upon human bodies. When they found in the woods hogs and flocks of sheep, or herds of cattle, they used to cut off the buttocks of the herdsmen, and the breasts of the women, looking upon those parts of the body as the greatest delicacy.'

But did the Romans ever visit Glasgow as such? Well, there are some remains, chiefly a Roman bowl of what is usually called

Roman milestone found at Old Kilpatrick.

Samian Ware but is actually from Gaul, found during excavations at Glasgow Green in the 1870s, plus the usual coins, pottery shards, inscribed stones and other Roman remains. These are now in the Hunterian Museum at the University of Glasgow.

At any event, the Romans went home properly after about AD 410, leaving nothing but an empty hole in the local economy where the wall-garrison soldiers had been. However, by that time the British Kingdom of Dumbarton was getting established, and the Christians had arrived.

A 'barbarian' captured by the Romans – who is not having a good time of it.

11

HERE COME THE CHRISTIANS

PATRICK, NINIAN AND KENTIGERN

Don't say so if there are any Irish listening, but St Patrick was quite possibly a local boy – hence 'Old Kilpatrick', literally 'Patrick's cell' ('cell' here meaning a hermit's dwelling or similar). He was born about AD 340, was captured by Irish slavers, escaped, but returned to Ulster as Bishop from AD 428 until his death in AD 440. Well, possibly – that would make him 100 years old! Patrick called his own birthplace 'the village of Bannavem of Tabernia' – but that's as clear as mud, and the subject of many a PhD and academic fist-fight ever since.

There is a stone of some antiquity in Kilpatrick churchyard with a figure supposedly representing Patrick himself; opposite, in the River Clyde, there was at one time a rock or small island called St Patrick's Stone, visible at low water. However, these are the sort of myths that arise later and get back-attributed, so we may never know.

More reliable is the arrival of St Ninian. He gets his first mention about 300 years after he must have lived. The story goes that he was from southern Scotland, or possibly Irish, but at any rate sent as an evangelising bishop to minister to what the Venerable Bede called the 'Southern Picts'. On the way he visited Tours, collected a few French stonemasons and built a white church, *Candida Casa*, at Whithorn,

St Patrick's Stone, looking across to Old Kilpatrick under the Erskine Bridge. This stone was either where the young Patrick was fishing when he was carried off to Ireland or a rock the Devil threw at him. Now it has a navigation light on it.

in around AD 397. On his travels, mostly to the east coast, he would have passed through Glasgow, and Bishop Jocelyn of Furness, actually writing in the late twelfth century about St Kentigern (below), mentions that Ninian had consecrated a cemetery where the cathedral and its burial ground now stand.

Kentigern is the next ecclesiast in the picture. A good way to start an argument in any Glasgow hostelry is to suggest that Kentigern and his sainted mother, Enoch, are actually from Fife. And if you're sitting comfortably, the story goes like this...

Over in the east – possibly in the land of King Leudonus or Lot, known as the 'half-pagan' (now the Lothians), or maybe in Northumbria – the daughter of that King was called Thenog or Thenew. She had visions of being a second Virgin Mary – as good an excuse as any to explain a surprise pregnancy. Her father found that a tad much, so he put his errant daughter to sea in a small boat. This beached at Culross on the Fife coast, where her son was born. Apparently, the child's father was Ewan (Owain) ap Urien, a prince of Strathclyde, or maybe King of Rheged, near modern Penrith in Cumbria. The boy was originally called 'Munghu', meaning 'dear' or 'beloved', which was later turned into Mungo. He was educated by Saint Serf, but quickly showed a penchant for miracles. One of these concerned a fire that Mungo had allowed to go out but re-lit by blowing on a frozen branch. Another was bringing a dead robin back to life after it was killed by jealous fellow students hoping to pin the blame on their teacher's favourite.

They were not best pleased at Mungo, and he had to leave Culross. He found refuge at the house of a holy man called Fergus. For whatever reason, Fergus died that night. Mungo loaded him onto a haycart which headed for Cathures, or

St Kentigern's statue at Kelvingrove museum, now facing to the back. There is a persistent rumour that the architect who designed the museum left the plans and went away, and came back to find it had been built the wrong way round. He shot himself. Great story, but none of it is correct – the road system was restructured, so the rear entrance had to be remodelled as the front.

Glasgow, stopping at a graveyard. Mungo had him interred in a spot later occupied by the south transept of the cathedral, which is still dedicated to Fergus.

Now that he was in Glasgu (supposedly the name Mungo gave it, meaning 'dear green place', 'dear family' or possibly the less poetic 'grey hollow'), he adopted or was given the local equivalent of his name, Kentigern, and set about putting his stamp on the place. There were a few demonstrations of his piety and gifts, so despite his youth (twenty-five years) the local King and clergy elected him bishop, and another bishop was brought from Ireland

The Glasgow coat of arms, referring to St Mungo's four 'miracles' – with the man himself in the crest.

to ordain him. He seems to have fallen out with a King Morken, though, and had to escape to an exile in Wales for twenty years where he had a nice time staying with St David. But, in around the year AD 573, there was a great battle at Ardderyd or Arthuret (shades of Arthurian mythology here!) between pagans and Christians, and Rydderch (Roderick) the Liberal became King of Strathclyde. Rydderch wanted the re-establishment of the Christian ways, so Kentigern returned with a company of 665 monks – making 666 of them in all, which must have put the willies up anyone who knew the Book of Revelations. This would have happened in about AD 582, we are told. He also met Saint Columba at Kilmacolm, as good a place as any.

Kentigern died on 13 January 603 (in his bath, according to Jocelyn), the same year as King Rydderch, who had made the mistake of staying over-long in Pertnech, or Partick, and both were buried in the church. Kentigern's mother became known as Enoch and is Glasgow's other patron saint.

Other miracles are attributed to Kentigern: apart from the kindling and the reanimated pet bird, he is said to have brought back a bell from the Pope in Rome (where he had reputedly gone on seven pilgrimages) and recovered a ring in the mouth of a Clyde salmon, a love token unwisely given away by King Rydderch's wife, Langueth, Queen of Cadzow (near Hamilton).

These stories are commemorated in the city's arms along with a line from a sermon he preached: 'Lord, Let Glasgow flourish by the preaching of the word and the praising of thy name', later abbreviated to 'Let Glasgow Flourish' and adopted as the city's motto.

However, the later city fathers (being of a Protestant bent and finding all this talk of miracles a bit Romish) instituted a poem taught to schoolchildren which essentially dismisses the marvels as myth:

Here is the bird that never flew
Here is the tree that never grew
Here is the bell that never rang
Here is the fish that never swam

Meanwhile, back in the Kingdom of Strathclyde...

AD 600-1200

THE FAIRLY DARK AGES

ACTUALLY, THE SO-CALLED 'Dark Ages' aren't nearly as 'dark' as the Roman-occupation period. It really isn't until 150 years after the Romans went back home to be sacked by a succession of Visigoths, Vandals and Huns that we can get any contemporary information about Glasgow and its surroundings. Clearly, Rydderch was the local Top Guy until AD 603. But, in the wider country, the Picts held the area north of the Forth; the Scotii from Ireland had established Dalriada in Argyll and were well-entrenched in the western isles; Anglo-Saxon settlers were in the east coast from Tweed to the Forth and getting a thumping from the Picts at Dunnichen in AD 685; but the Britons still had the old Roman province, including Strathclyde, with its capital at Alt Cluyd (Dumbarton), and possibly exerting control through Dumfriesshire as far south as the Derwent in Cumberland.

In AD 756, though, the Strathclyde Britons surrendered to an alliance between Eadbert, King of Northumbria, and Angus, King of the Picts, and they took Alt Cluyd, torching it in 780. Kenneth MacAlpin had a fairly good go at uniting Scot-Gael, Pict, Anglian and Briton into Alba (Scotland) in AD 835, largely (and allegedly) by inviting all his Pictish rivals to dinner and murdering them. Some host. In AD 875 it was the turn of the Danes to have a bash at the Picts and the Strathclyders, by now often referred to as 'Cumbrian' or 'Welsh' as their languages were essentially the same.

The *Saxon Chronicle* tells us that in AD 945 Edmund of Wessex, as if it was any of his business, gave 'all Cumbraland' (meaning northern England as well as Strathclyde) to Malcolm, King of Scots. The Strathclyders were openly hostile to the Kings of Scots right up till Owen the Bald, the last real King of Strathclyde, died in AD 1018, leaving the road open to Malcolm II to sign up his own grandson (also Malcolm) as the successor client-king.

By this time, various incorporated trades in Glasgow were being established and recognised by charter – probably the first were the masons, wrights and coopers in 1057, during the time of Malcolm III, which suggests considerable commercial enterprise was taking place.

It was the return from England of David – who was Earl of Huntingdon by virtue of his marriage to the Saxon Countess Matilda – as King of Scots that truly united

Scotland under feudal law, in 1124. There was considerable immigration of Anglo-Normans, who were given lands (or at least, the bits not taken as royal demesnes or granted to the Church). David's tutor had been consecrated John, Bishop of Glasgow, some time before 1118.

At this point in history, the area that included Glasgow, Partick and Govan was a royal demesne, under the Earl-Prince (later King) David, who had his palace at Rutherglen. But the Church also had (or acquired) considerable properties, with the bishop as their landlord. Later raised to a barony, the name survives in that of the parish surrounding the cathedral. The importance of Rutherglen is clear in a charter of William towards the end of the century confirming that David had erected it to the status of a Royal Burgh, exercising customs and other duties over the whole Glasgow area.

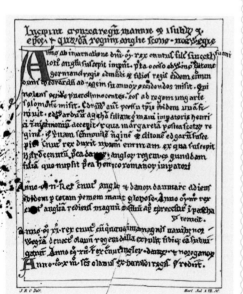

The Chronicles of the Kings of Mann and the Isles (Chronica Regum Manniæ et Insularum or Manx Chronicle), written in medieval Latin at the Cistercian Rushen Abbey in around 1261.

Of course, a powerful bishop needs a big cathedral, so in 1123 David gave £5 a year to help out. A lot of money in those days. David added to this wealth by granting land in 'Perthec' and 'Guven' to 'the church of St Kentigern of Glasgow and the bishopric'.

All of this set the stage for another stooshie. Walter FitzAllan, Steward of Scotland (and thus progenitor of the Stewarts) held what we would now call Renfrew. The Church was gathering in more lands, money and power. While Henry I, David's brother-in-law, was on the throne of England, relations were peaceable. But in 1136 Stephen ignored a settlement that gave the English crown to King Henry's daughter, Maud (Matilda), and David naturally leapt to the defence of his niece, a fight which lasted years. In the process he took a lot of the north of England between the Eden and the Tees.

But the next King of Scots, a very young Malcolm IV, had to give these up, setting the Scottish border more or less where it is now, and falling out with Henry II of England. He also had a fight on his hands at home, against revolts by the powerful petty Kings of Strathearn, Moray and Galloway – and the big beast of his day, Somerled, Lord of the Isles and of Argyll. David had died in 1153, as had King Olaf of the Isle of Man, so in 1164, seeing the main chance, Somerled led an army of Western Isles men and Irishmen, with 160 ships, to attack Glasgow and Renfrew, where Walter FitzAllan was just putting up the last wallpaper in his new castle.

We know some of what happened next because of a poem on the death of Somerled, written by a Glasgow cleric called William, and the *Chronicles of the Kings of Mann and the Isles*, composed about a century later. The invasion fleet landed on the Clyde shore near Inchinnan and headed for Renfrew, right through the territory of the Stewarts.

They took the hump, naturally, leading to the Battle of Renfrew. At least, we think so – there is a fair bit of confusion over whether it happened at all. If it did, it was the home team (the army of Malcolm IV of Scotland led by Walter FitzAlan and Herbert, Bishop of Glasgow) *vs* the forces of Somerled, the King of Mann and the Isles and the King of Argyll, Cinn Tìre (Kintyre) and Lorne – 15,000 of them and an armada of 160 birlinns or lymphads, their version of the Viking longship.

Somerled's warriors were no match for the mounted knights and armoured men of the Scots, and Somerled was wounded in the leg by a javelin. He was then attacked and killed by the swordsmen, along with his eldest son, Gillecallum. Or perhaps, as some accounts have it, he was assassinated in his tent by a page (who then cut off Somerled's head and took it to King Malcolm as a wee present, according to the *Book of Clanranald*). Whatever really brought about his death, the Gaelic-Celtic-Viking army, suddenly without a leader, fled through the Tuchen Woods: many were slaughtered as they ran, and the survivors took off in their ships. The peoples of the Western Isles became part of Scotland, but have been a bit temperamental about it ever since.

Because Somerled and his son were killed in a battle led by the Bishop of Glasgow, everyone credited St Kentigern with assuring the victory from upon high. So that's all right then. It was this bishop – Herbert of Selkirk by name, although he was a foreigner – who started writing a *Life of St Kentigern*, copied and expanded by Jocelyn some twenty-five years later.

A rather idealised image of a Lord of the Isles from the time of Somerled.

There used to be an octagonal monument in a field near the Knock, erected by Walter FitzAlan at the site of the battle (and rather cheekily he had a seal made in 1170 showing himself leaning against it) but it was taken away in 1779, for some obscure reason.

The other consequence of Somerled's defeat was that a later Walter Stewart, the 6th High Steward of Scotland (*b.* 1292) married Marjorie Bruce, daughter of King Robert Bruce, in 1315, and in 1371 their son became Robert II, considered to be the first Stewart King.

'STOCK IT WELL WITH ENGLISH HEADS':

William Wallace and the Bell O' The Brae

EVERYONE TALKS ABOUT the battles of Falkirk, Stirling Bridge and Bannockburn, but as far as Glasgow was concerned the whole Wars of Independence were waged at the Battle of the Bell o' the Brae. Blind Harry the Minstrel wrote (or someone wrote for him) a metrical epic describing how William Wallace thrashed a troop of English in the streets of Glasgow.

Just so we're clear here, Sir William Wallace was a nearly local boy; his family hailed from Ellerslie or Elderslie, just across the Clyde from Glasgow, and his uncle was possibly Abbot of Paisley. Mel Gibson's *Braveheart* often comes in for a pasting, but it did a better job of getting some historical reality into Hollywood than many movies (*Brave*, for example!).

He came to prominence when Scotland made the tactical blunder of asking Edward I of England to referee the argument between the factions of Bruce and Balliol/Comyn in 1292 over who would be King of Scots after the death of Alexander III's granddaughter, Margaret, Maid of Norway, who had contracted a fatal dose of yellow fever on her way home. John Balliol won the toss and was crowned, but renounced his enforced homage to Edward in 1296, leading to a series of punitive strikes at Berwick and Dunbar, hostage-taking and the abdication of Balliol in Edward's favour. Wallace, who probably had some military training and was certainly a big, strong lad (but not the 7ft giant of poetic legend), went on a controlled rampage, first killing William de Heselrig, the English High Sheriff of Lanark, raiding Scone with William Douglas the Hardy, and joining with other guerrilla uprisings when the Scots nobles capitulated at Irvine in July 1296.

The minstrel Blind Harry recounts that Wallace, infuriated by the surrender, was on his way from Ayr 'to Glaskow bryg, that byggit was of tre' (with a wooden bridge), later called 'Wallace's Brig', replaced in 1833 by 'the Bridge of Sighs'. It was culverted forty years later to become Ladywell Street. The laird of Auchinleck took half of the 300 horsemen across the Clyde elsewhere, 'for he the pasage kend', while Wallace marched his company over the wooden bridge and up what is now High Street to the Bishop's Castle, roughly where the Royal Infirmary now stands. At precisely the right moment, Auchinleck stormed in by 'the north-east Raw' (Drygait) in a pincer movement. In the brief but bloody encounter that followed, the commander, Earl Percy, was killed (by Wallace personally, it was said). The legend goes that the English garrison's soldiers, who had terrorised Glasgow, were beheaded and Wallace, pointing to a well, declared 'stock it well with English heads' – which accounts for the name 'Stockwell Street'. Nonsense!

The remainder of the 1,000-strong English force fled via the woods beyond Blackfriars' Kirk to Bothwell Castle, which had been a Moray stronghold but was now where the English were headquartered. Blind Harry says:

> Out off the gait die byschope Beik thai
>   lede,
> For than thaim thocht it was no tyme to
>   bide,
> By the Frer Kyrk, til a worde fast besyde.
> In that forest, forsuth, thai taryit nocht;
> On fresche horss to Bothwell sone thai
>   socht.
> Wallace followed with worthie men and
>   wicht.

Engraving of the famous picture of Wallace's trial at Westminster, painted by Irish artist Daniel Maclise (1806-1870).

The 'byschope Beik' referred to Bishop Beck, and his flight certainly didn't impress King Edward, who wrote: 'Anthony is on his travels'. Bothwell Castle, occupied by the English, withstood a siege by the Scots for over than a year before being starved into surrender. The Scots held it until it was recaptured by the English late in 1301 in a momentous siege. Edward, living up to his 'Hammer of the Scots' reputation, brought almost 7,000 soldiers and hauled a great siege tower called 'the belfry' from Glasgow. The inside ladders allowed the attacking forces onto the castle battlements, from where they hacked and slashed their way into the castle keep. The Scots surrendered within the month.

Probably just to rub salt into the wound, Edward went into Glasgow and made his devotions at various altars and important shrines, including that of St Kentigern. Edward also burned the monastery at Paisley, as a punishment for the monks' loyalty to Wallace. The message was 'I can do what I want in this country'. But, as Glaswegians say, 'Oh, d'ye think so?' To repair Bothwell Castle he had to buy timber, coal, iron, implements and furniture, hire waggoners and pay for food, guards and storage, thereby putting a lot of money into local purses.

However, back in 1297, after the siege of Dundee in early September, Wallace and his ally from the north, Andrew Moray, led an army to the Stirling Bridge where the outnumbered Scottish army made mincemeat of John de Warenne's 3,000 cavalry and 10,000 infantry, using a series of clever tactics like forcing them to cross a narrow bridge and taking the pegs out, and using shiltroms (a defensive pallisade of sharpened wooden stakes) to force the English foot-soldiers back into their own cavalry.

High Street in around 1905, a mere 607 years after Wallace rode up here for the Battle of Bell o' the Brae.

SKIN THE TREASURY!

During the battle, Edward's treasurer, Hugh Cressingham, was killed. His skin was flayed off and cut into pieces as a victory token, with Wallace himself using 'a broad strip… taken from the head to the heel' to make a sword-belt, as the *Lanercost Chronicle* tells us.

Wallace and Moray became guardians of the kingdom of Scotland on behalf of the worthless John Balliol, but Moray died of wounds later that year. Wallace then raided Northumberland and Cumberland and was knighted.

The English retaliated, winning the Battle of Falkirk in 1298. Wallace went abroad – to drum up support, it is assumed – and came back in 1304 to get involved again in the fighting. However, he was tricked by Sir John de Menteith, governor of Dumbarton Castle (and, some say, with the collusion of Robert Bruce), who captured Wallace at Robroyston near Glasgow and turned him over to the English. Because of 'Fause Menteith's' treachery, Loch Menteith is known to this day as Lake Menteith, the only lake in Scotland. Wyntoun's *Metrical Chronicle* of 1418 tells us:

Schyre Jhon of Menteith in tha days
Tuk in Glasgow William Walays;
And sent hym until Ingland sune,
There was he quartayrd and undone.

Wallace was taken to Westminster Hall in London, tried for treason and atrocities against civilians, crowned with a garland of oak (indicating he was 'King of Outlaws'), convicted – to no one's surprise – and then stripped and dragged naked at the heels of a horse to Smithfield, where he was hanged, drawn and quartered.

This particularly barbaric triad of punishments involved hanging the victim until he was strangled but still alive. He was then castrated, his bowels pulled out and burnt before his eyes, beheaded, and the rest of his body cut into four parts. Wallace's head was preserved in tar and stuck on a pike at London Bridge. His other four parts were sent to Newcastle upon Tyne, Berwick, Perth and Stirling, where they were displayed.

This was not to be the end of the matter, however. In early 1306 Robert Bruce again started a campaign, and the fight for Scottish independence went on, culminating at Bannockburn in 1314. Scots are very proud of that one, as it was more or less our last Home Win.

PLAGUE, PLAGUE AND PLAGUE AGAIN

GLASGOW HAS SUFFERED its share of plagues, including what are known as the Three Pestilences: First (1350), Second (1362), and Third (1381). The pestilence that raged through Scotland in 1350 was the Black Death, which had arrived, probably at Bristol, two years earlier in its bubonic form as transmitted by rat-fleas, transforming itself by that winter into the even more devastating air-borne pneumonic version. The next two epidemics were not quite so devastating, as there was now some residual immunity in the population.

Although rats get the blame, and then the fleas on the rats, the real culprit is the bacterium *Yersinia pestis*. It started out in China, moved along the Silk Road to the Crimea by 1346, spread via merchant ships throughout the Mediterranean area and the rest of Europe and killed possibly 60 per cent of the European population – leading indirectly to the Peasant's Revolt of 1351.

The first person we know to describe the plague and the suppurating buboes it caused in the neck, groin and armpits was Boccaccio in his *Decameron* – and he knew what he was talking about, as he watched it kill about three quarters of the population in his native Florence in 1348. 'In men and women alike,' he wrote, 'it first betrayed itself by the emergence of certain tumours in the groin or armpits, some of which grew as large as a common apple, others as an egg.'

It's a shame that St Roche wasn't still about, as during his lifetime (1295-1327) he was said to have provided miraculous cures to those affected by the plague. However, by 1501 Glasgow had a church at Stable Green port dedicated to him, and its extensive burial grounds were used to inhume the plague victims, then and later. His expected intercession doesn't seem to have had much effect, though – as Glasgow grew, with all the attendant overcrowding and filth, it was inevitable that there would be further epidemics.

In 1498 Glasgow instigated a forty-day quarantine for anyone wishing to enter the city without permission of the council, the penalty being confiscation of all goods plus banishment. In 1574 and 1584 plagues ravaged Glasgow again. Then, in 1588, it was time for Glasgow to get its own back – a plague hit Paisley and nearby Kilmacolm. Travel from Glasgow was forbidden, as was trade with these places.

The Dance of Death, from the Nuremberg Chronicles.

On 17 April 1600, the Kirk Session was so worried about plague – or 'glengore', as they called it – that they 'sent to the council to deplore the infection that is in this city by the glengore, and some to convene again in the Blackfriars Kirk anent it, and the whole chirurgeons and professors of medicine in town to be present.'

In 1644-48 there were more epidemics, the earliest possibly stemming from Scottish soldiers returning from a battle at Newcastle. The magistrates of Glasgow issued a proclamation on 9 November 1644 putting the blame firmly on the Almighty: 'As it hath pleased God', they recorded, 'to visit the south country with the plague of pestilence...'. However, it did make an English commander, sent to take Glasgow, think twice about even entering the city. Good for the plague!

In 1647 Glasgow University had to evacuate to Irvine, Ayrshire. This time St Roche came into his own, as the burying-ground of the chapel dedicated to him (now called St Rollox) was used to receive the poor who were infected. The 'Deacon of the Gardeners' died of plague in 1649, and all his papers were destroyed as a precaution, including the original charter of the trade.

That was more or less the end of plague in Glasgow – except for an outbreak

Homo natus de muliere, breui viuens tempore, repletur multis miserijs: qui quasi flos egreditur & conteritur & fugit velut vmbra

Death made off with the young as their distraught parents lit fires to keep the pestilence at bay. (With the kind permission of the Thomas Fisher Rare Book Library, Library of Toronto)

in August 1900, which killed sixteen people. Estimates of the dead in previous outbreaks are either not available or unreliable – it seems everyone was too busy burying and trying not to breathe in to make a proper headcount.

Of course, there was always leprosy. This disease has a worse reputation than it deserves. The infection (by *Mycobacterium leprae*) leads to pale patches on the skin; these are usually painless and not itchy, so are often ignored. The bacterium concerned prefers life a bit colder than core body temperature, so it tends to thrive at the extremities: the hands, feet and tip of the nose, typically. As the disease progresses, there is nerve damage and other complications, producing a lack of sensation at the affected points. Because they are not painful, the wounds get ignored and fester

– hence the characteristic deformities of the limbs and face. The eaten-away faces and limbs of the afflicted led to a stigma against sufferers and their exclusion from normal society. Bad diet and lack of proper hygiene as a consequence of poverty didn't help, but even the rich caught it – Robert Bruce died of it. However, leprosy isn't all that easy to catch – it is less contagious than the common cold, and you'd have to live for some years in an area where it is endemic to catch it. Most of us would rather not, though. Almost every part of Europe had endemic leprosy from the tenth to the sixteenth centuries, which then gradually disappeared.

In Glasgow – or rather, just outside of it – lepers were confined to St Ninian's Hospital at Brigend, safely across on the Southside, which later became the Gorbals. Lepers could enter Glasgow on two days a week provided they covered their faces with muslin, kept away from everyone and rang a clapper-bell. An ordinance of 25 October 1586, reinforced on 9 December, 'put all Lepers out of Town for fear of infection like to rise by it'.

The story of leprosy in Glasgow goes back before that, though: St Mungo 'cleansed' lepers (or so Jocelyn tells us), and they were also healed at Mungo's tomb. On a more practical note, Glasgow had taken the care of lepers as a legal obligation from the start, as did most Royal Burghs. An old burghal law provided that lepers who could maintain themselves would be put into the hospital. For paupers, the burgesses were to collect money for their food and clothing. A later ordinance refers to alms collected 'for the sustenance of lepers in a proper place outwith the burgh', as they were not allowed to solicit door-to-door but could sit 'at the toune's end and beg alms from any entering or leaving Glasgow'. They also had to carry their own drinking cups.

It was a matter of Church law (following a Bull of Pope Alexander III in the late 1100s) that every leprosarium should have its own churchyard, chapel and clerics. This wasn't so much an act of kindness as a consequence of barring lepers from worshipping in churches and being buried in churchyards other than their own. Today we would call that a Public Health measure. The Gorbals' hospital had its own cemetery and grounds, plus a chapel about 100 yards to the south, possibly replacing an older building when it was built in about 1490 by William Steward, a canon of the cathedral. He also endowed a chaplaincy with rents from properties on the Southside and in the city, and on the anniversary of his death each year twenty-four poor scholars were to be paid one penny each to celebrate certain services, half of which went to the lepers, who rang the chapel bell for the *Salve Regina* every night and prayed in thanks.

The usual deal was that you were expected to give alms every time that you travelled in or out of Glasgow, a bit like a toll. King James IV, for example, coming to Glasgow from Kilmarnock in 1497, gave two shillings 'to the seke folk at the brig of Glasgo' and when leaving for Stirling a further three shillings 'to the pur folk in Glasgo', followed on another occasion by two shillings 'to the seke folk in the grantgore, at the toune end of Glasgo'. The 'grantgore' is the same as 'glengore', or plague, mentioned above.

If you used that entry regularly, it was better to give a regular endowment – so, for instance, the Bishops of Glasgow gave annually two bolls of meal (a boll was about 140lb or 60kg) but the monks of Paisley trumped them with six bolls.

Leper hospitals are often known as 'Lazar houses', a reference to St Lazarus, the patron saint of lepers, identified with the beggar Lazarus from Luke 19:19-31 (not the Lazarus raised from the dead in the Gospel of John). So many knights visiting Palestine during the crusades contracted the disease that there had to be a special Military and Hospitaller Order established some time before 1142 to look after them. It survives today as the Order of St Lazarus of Jerusalem and is still involved with the disease.

Mind you, there were other theories of the origins of leprosy, plague and other contagions, which help explain why everyone was so keen to have lepers buried outside town. One was that it was spread by the undead: they allegedly feasted on corpses and spread pestilence that way. In 2009, on the island of Lazzaretto Nuovo ('the new Leper-House'), in the lagoon of Venice, the remains of a female 'vampire' were uncovered in a mass grave dating from the 1576 Black Death epidemic. She had been buried with a brick jammed in her mouth to stop her feeding on other victims, as reported in Glasgow's very own *Scottish Daily Record*.

AD 1568

THE BATTLE OF LANGSIDE

IF THERE WAS ever a 'Hundred Years' War' in Scotland, it was around the issues of religion. The Protestant Reformation had happened in the early 1560s, and it set in motion a series of wars – civil, and against England – that would beggar Scotland and set up a religious divide still felt today, especially in Glasgow and the west. There were other problems too – in 1563 there was 'a grit dearth approaching to a famine', for example. However, on the bright side, in 1569 an alcohol-pricing policy set the cost of wine at 18 pence a pint, and ale at 4 pence a pint – the same as a 32oz loaf.

One of the most bloody and infamous events of the era was the Battle of Langside. On 13 May 1568, Mary Queen of Scots lost a mêlée, less than a mile south of Glasgow's centre, against her half-brother, Regent Moray (James Stewart, 1st Earl of Moray c.1531-1570, one of the many illegitimate children of James V). She then lost her crown, her freedom and ultimately her head.

Moray was based in Glasgow, and Mary's army came from Hamilton along the south bank of the Clyde. The Queen's party of 6,000 was trying to reach Dumbarton Castle, where Mary would be safe, by fording the Clyde at Dalmarnock. Moray got there first, so Mary marched along the southern bank – only to find the Regent had crossed Stockwell Bridge at Glasgow with his 4,000 troops. He also had with him Sir William Kirkcaldy of Grange, said to be the most able soldier in Europe. Kirkcaldy later became the

One lesson everyone learned at Langside was how daft it was to go into battle covered with heavy armour. The fighting men were so overweighted that they could hardly wield their weapons, and in any case it was almost impossible to sustain or to deal a serious wound, which rather defeats the point of a sword fight…

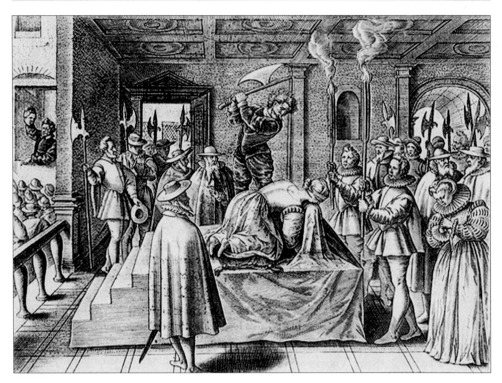

The beheading of Mary Queen of Scots on 8 February 1587 was badly botched. The headsman had three goes at it without severing the Queen's head, and had to saw though the skin and muscles with his knife. Then he picked up her head – and her wig came off. They had to physically prise her pet dog – blood-soaked and distraught – away from her. Mary had hidden it under her skirt, for some reason, and the executioners found it while trying to pull off her garters. One question is often asked: does beheading hurt? Well, Mary gave a long groan after the first axe-stroke, so it probably does. A contemporary account says, 'Her lips stirred up and down a quarter of an hour after her head was cut off'.

Queen's last and greatest champion, defending Edinburgh Castle for her cause and losing his head in the process.

Moray arranged his troops on Langside Hill, while Mary's were on the smaller Clincart Hill (now the site of Langside College, a half mile to the east), and the Queen watched from Cathcart Hill (now called Court Knowe). There was an ineffective cavalry charge, after which Mary's infantry marched on Langside Hill – where they were met by gunfire, and Moray's soldiers coming downhill. The fighting that ensued was vicious: the 5th Lord Home (sometimes spelt Hume), for example, who fought against Mary at the battle, 'on foot, with his pike in his hand, very manfully... [was] stricken to the ground by many strokes upon his face, through the throwing [of] pistols at him after they had been discharged. He was also wounded with staves, and had many strokes of spears through his legs.'

The Regent's men proved hard to drive out of the streets and gardens of the Langside village. Having pinned Mary's army between the two onslaughts, Moray deployed his archers, then infantry, followed by cavalry. Only 100 (some say 300) of Mary's troops were killed,

Monument at the site.

Hill: its paw rests on a cannonball. More to the point, Moray was so pleased with the bread the Corporation of Bakers had provided to his army that he gifted them the Burrowfield lands where he had encamped, and this became the Patrick Mills or Bunhouse, and later the Regent Flour Mills.

DEATH TO THE REGENT!

For the victory at Langside, and for running Scotland rather well, Moray managed to bring about peace in civil life and in the Church, which accounts for his nickname 'The Good Regent'. However, he didn't get much of a chance to enjoy his success. On 23 January, James Hamilton of Bothwellhaugh, a supporter of Mary and a nephew of Archbishop John Hamilton, used a brass match-lock rifled carbine to shoot and fatally wound Moray from his uncle's house as Moray was passing by. This is the first-ever assassination by a gun on record.

Moray's body was taken to Leith. It then continued to Holyrood and subsequently to St Giles, where he was buried in St Anthony's aisle on 14 February. Seven lords carried the casket. Sir William Kirkcaldy of Grange held Moray's standard and John Knox preached. His wife, Agnes, was buried in the tomb on her death in 1588, and was succeeded by his eldest daughter, who married her distant cousin, James Stewart (who became 2nd Earl of Moray on their marriage). This Moray was murdered by the Marquess of Huntly in 1592, an act so unpopular that King James VI, fearing a rebellion, chose to leave Edinburgh and hide in Glasgow. Huntly received a week's house arrest in Blackness Castle as his punishment for the murder.

and 400 captured, but that was enough to make the rest of them turn tail, and Mary herself headed for England and into the clutches of Queen Elizabeth. Bad move! It might have gone better for her if she had been captured when her horse got stuck briefly in a bog called Moll's Mire. The whole battle had taken less than an hour. After the disastrous outcome, the Queen's party, time and time again, occupied Glasgow in considerable number, headed by Argyle and Hamilton. But Moray completed his retribution against the Hamiltons for their support of the Queen by later burning to the ground their castle at nearby Rutherglen.

There is now a memorial at Langside, with a lion on top facing towards Clincart

AD 1617

THE EXECUTION OF SAINT JOHN OGILVIE

THE YEARS AFTER the Reformation had been a bit... well, robust! In 1577 an assassin had tried to kill John Knox. One of Queen Mary's soldiers tried – but failed – to stab John Craig in church, and the Assembly of that year saw John Anderson on his knees and asking forgiveness of the Church for thumping Robert Boyd, minister of Newtyle, 'to the effusion of blood'. John Howieson, minister of Cambuslang and moderator of Glasgow Presbytery, had a meeting broken up by the Burgh authorities and was pulled by the beard, hit in the face so that a tooth fell out and banged up in the Tolbooth by the provost. The Earl of Montrose, another provost of Glasgow, manhandled David Wemis out of the cathedral pulpit. Three short years later, the same Wemis had to draw his own short sword (interesting that he had one on him) to defend himself against a father and son called Cunningham, who attacked him with blows, sword and pistol and called him a liar. Fortunately, however, Andrew Hay, parson of Renfrew, was also going equipped, and arrived in time to draw his knife and make a stand alongside his friend. The Church Militant indeed!

Time to formalise things, then – so in 1581 the 'Negative Confession of Faith', with the National Covenant attached, denounced the Pope and the Roman Catholic Church in no uncertain terms. In Glasgow, 2,250 people signed it, which must have been almost the entire adult population. The Negative Confession (also known as the King's Confession) had been drawn up by order of James VI and it was a rip-snorter! It contains lines like:

We abhor and detest all contrary Religion and Doctrine; but chiefly all kinds of Papistry in general...

We detest and refuse the usurped authority of that Roman Antichrist upon the scriptures of God, upon the Kirk, the civil Magistrate, and consciences of men...

[We refute the] blasphemous opinion of transubstantiation, or real presence of Christ's body in the elements, and receiving of the same by the wicked...

[We refute the] worshipping of imagery, relics, and crosses; dedicating of kirks, altars, days; vows to creatures...
[We refute] praying or speaking in a strange language [meaning Latin]

ler.5o.5. Come let us joyn ourselves to the Lord

i 6   a Solemn.   4 3   in a perpetuall Covenant that shall not be forgotten.

LEAGVE AND COVENANT,
for Reformation, and defence of Religion, the Honour and happinesse of the king, and the Peace and safety, of the three kingdoms of

ENGLAND, SCOTLAND, and IRELAND.

We Noblemen, Barons, Knights, Gentlemen, Citizens, Burgesses, Ministers of the Gospel, and Commons of all forts in the Kingdoms of England, Scotland, and Ireland, by the Providence of God living under one King, and being of one reformed Religion, having before our eyes the Glory of God, and the advancement of the Kingdome of our Lord and Saviour Iesus Christ, the Honour and happinesse of the kings Majesty and his posterity, and the true publique Liberty, Safety, and Peace of the Kingdoms, wherein every ones private Condition is included, and calling to minde the treacherous and bloody Plots, Conspiracies, Attempts, and Practices of the Enemies of God, against the true Religion, and professors thereof in all places, especially in these three kingdoms ever since the Reformation of Religion, and how much their rage, power and presumption, are of late, and at this time increased and exercised; whereof the deplorable state of the Church and kingdom of Ireland, the distressed estate of the Church and kingdom of England, and the dangerous estate of the Church and kingdom of Scotland, are present and publique Testimonies; We have now at last, (after other means of Supplication, Remonstrance, Protestations, and Sufferings) for the preservation of our selves and our Religion, from utter Ruine and Destruction; according to the commendable practice of these Kingdoms in former times, and the Example of Gods people in other Nations; After mature deliberation, resolved and determined to enter into a mutuall and solemn Legue and Covenant; wherein we all subscribe, and each one of us for himself, with our hands lifted up to the most high God, do sweare;

Many are stirred up by Satan, and that Roman Antichrist, to promise, swear, subscribe, and for a time use the holy sacraments in the kirk deceitfully, against their own conscience...

Stirring stuff – and a nail in the coffin to Roman Catholicism in Scotland. At a General Assembly at Glasgow that year, Presbyteries were established, Episcopacy was doomed and the kirk claimed its own jurisdiction, free of control by the State or the King.

The Glasgow Kirk Session took the Reformed religion seriously – in 1587 they set penalties for immorality, including fines, being carted through the town, ducked in the Clyde, and put in stocks or on the 'cuckstool' at Glasgow Cross. The next year the session banned 'exercise' in Blackfriars' church on Fridays and made everyone assemble for Sunday communion at four in the morning. By 1608 they had forbidden certain things on the Sabbath – meetings of women, selling of alcohol and buying of timber. Women, incidentally, were also not allowed to sit on the benches in church but had to bring a stool and bare their heads.

Scotland's only post-Reformation saint offended these rules, and was martyred in 1615 as a consequence. John Ogilvie was born in Scotland of nobility in 1589, and brought up as a Presbyterian. His father sent him to the France for education, thinking John Calvin's country would keep him on the right track. John, though, became unconvinced by Calvinism and, because he could speak a number of languages, was able to consult with German and Italian Catholic scholars who talked him out of the Protestant Reformation as it had divided the Church, in contravention of God's will that all

SINS AMONGST THE CLERGY

We shouldn't forget that many clerics had actually entered the Church for an easy life and a secure livelihood, and not because of any particular principles. The Reformation must have come as a shock to them, as the kirk sought not only to purify the faithful but also to weed out the immoralities of its ministers. The incumbents at Jedburgh and Kilspindie were ousted for leading scandalous lives and in 1570 John Kello, minister of Spott near Dunbar, was executed for wife-strangling.

Crimes and Sufferings of the Scottish Clergy from 1560 till 1690

The following list is taken from Appendix VIII of *The Covenanters, A History of the Church in Scotland from the Reformation to the Revolution* by James King Hewison, 1908. How many people these days get 'fugitated'?

FROM	1560-1638	1635-1660	1660-1690
Executed:	2	1	8 (laity 197)
Murdered:	2	4	2
Killed:	1	2	3
Imprisoned:	31	21	78
Banished or fugitated:	18	13	17
Deposed:	35	126	46
Deprived:	14	12	548
Suspended:	3	7	4
Outed and rabbled:	1	3	142
OFFENCES FOR WHICH THEY SUFFERED			
Immorality:	11	11	21
Scandalous irregularities and ministerial insufficiency:	18	15	15
Murder:	2	1	1
Petty offences:	16	15	13
Witchcraft:	…	3	…
Political offences:	40	80	22
Drunkenness:	2	12	32
Nonconformity to Episcopacy (Presbyterianism):	34	5	275
Nonconformity to Presbytery (Episcopacy) and adoption of the liturgy:	14	70	345
The test:	…	…	45

In 1538 religious persecution was rife in Scotland and cities vied with each other as to who could burn the most heretics. The Archbishop of Glasgow – who was, of course, the famous Gavin Dunbar – was keen to top the First Division, so he went looking for victims. He quickly found some. In 1528, Dunbar had signed the sentence of Patrick Hamilton, who was then burned alive for six hours before dying (the faggots were wet), so becoming one of the Scottish Reformation's most famous martyrs. Dunbar was made Chancellor of Scotland.

In 1538 he got hold of Jerome Russell, a Franciscan friar, and Alexander Kennedy, who, although only eighteen years old, had distinguished himself as a poet and, some said, a genius, and five other victims. They were brought to trial in Glasgow before the bishop's court, where Russell said:

> This is your hour and power of darkness; now sit ye as judges, and we stand wrongfully accused, and more wrongfully to be condemned; but the day shall come when our innocency shall appear, and that ye shall see your own blindness to your everlasting confusion. Go forward and fulfil the measure of your iniquity.

Then they went to the stake. Bishop Dunbar went on to greater heights in 1543 when he physically attacked Cardinal Archbishop David Beaton.

men are to be saved and to come to the knowledge of the truth. John Calvin had taught that God wants certain people to get to Heaven and quite frankly doesn't want certain others, so not everyone will receive His grace. So Ogilvie became a Catholic at Lorraine in 1597 and – despite being thrown out by the Jesuits – persevered with the Benedictines, then had another shot at the Society of Jesus, this time in Austria. He was sent to France – what better place for a re-converted Protestant? – but decided he could do good back in Scotland.

Then Ogilvie returned home in 1613, disguised as a retired soldier and horse trader and calling himself John Watson. He had specifically asked to be sent to Glasgow to minister to the few remaining Catholics there, who mainly met in private. He got to know a widow, Marian Walker, who sheltered priests, allowed them to celebrate Mass, hear confessions, administer the sacraments and so on, and later died in prison, considered a martyr by Catholics to this day.

Less than a year later, Ogilvie was informed on by Adam Boyd, an agent of the Protestant Archbishop of Glasgow, John Spottiswoode, and on 14 October he was arrested, imprisoned in the Archbishop's palace and taken before the Glasgow Burgh Court, followed by Paisley gaol – where a dreadful fate awaited him. He was carrying little but a confessor's catechism, a form of dispensation, and a lock of hair from St Ignatius Loyola, founder of the Jesuits. Ogilvie was tried twice. At the first, he was told that it was a capital crime in Scotland to offer Mass. 'Prove it,' he replied. They couldn't, so they dropped that particular charge. They then asked him why he came to Scotland. He replied, 'to un-teach heresy and to save souls', which did not go down well at all.

Ogilvie's torture lasted five months after his arrest. He was beaten, and his fingernails were pulled out with pliers. He was subjected to both threats and bribery, starved and deprived of sleep – all tortures designed to reveal the names of those who had sheltered him. He was moved to Edinburgh for a time, for investigation by the Privy Council, and in particular was subjected to 'the vigil' or sleep deprivation, originally designed to elicit confessions of witchcraft. Victims of this torture were punched, kicked and pierced with pins and other sharp instruments. The device known as the 'witch's bridle' was also applied. Spottiswoode wanted to apply the 'torture of the boots', which involved a rawhide sock soaked in water, pulled over the foot and lower leg and bound in place

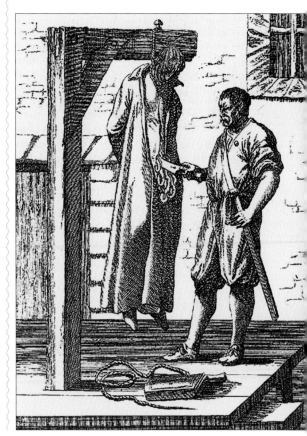

with cords, then slowly heated over a fire to make the hide contract, squeezing the foot until the bones become dislocated. In the end, however, this torture was not used on Ogilvie.

After almost nine days and nights of the 'vigil', he was at death's door. They let him rest and then brought him back in front of the council. Ogilvie still refused to compromise, even when offered 'a rich provostry' – in other words, the bribe of a substantial living.

Ogilvie kept appealing to the crown, and King James – whom he had met in London – sent him five rather loaded questions to answer, but Ogilvie just repeated: 'So far as civil obedience goes, the King does not have a more obedient subject in his realms, but in matters of the spirit, King James has no jurisdiction.'

King James begged to differ – he considered himself Head of Absolutely Everything, with a divine right to rule, a feeling bolstered when he inherited Henry VIII's Church of England in 1603, and he wasn't going to be lectured by an upstart Glasgow Jesuit. The King said Ogilvie should repudiate 'the Bishop of Rome' (the Pope) or die. Finally, he was tried for treason on 10 March 1615, at Glasgow's Tolbooth. The judge and jury took a surprisingly long two hours to find him guilty, and he was sentenced to be hanged and quartered the same afternoon.

Ogilvie spent three hours in prayer (the court was having lunch!) before the sheriff took him to the scaffold. There was a final promise of a royal pardon and a substantial reward, but the priest merely prayed with his rosary, again declared his loyalty to the King, and said that he was dying for the sake of 'religion alone'. Ogilvie threw his rosary into the crowd, where it hit a visiting Hungarian merchant – who was converted on the spot. The city hangman tied Ogilvie's hands, guided him up the ladder and pushed him off, speeding his demise by pulling on his legs. Public feeling was riding high at the injustice of the whole affair, and so the body was not quartered but quietly taken away to be buried amongst criminals outside the city. John Ogilvie was thirty-six years old.

In 1929 he was beatified, becoming the Blessed John Ogilvie, but almost immediately the campaign started to have him declared a saint. That requires a miracle, of course, so it was handy that in 1967 a Glasgow dockyard worker called John Fagan, who lived in the parish named after Father Ogilvie, suddenly recovered from cancer and told his wife he was hungry – having lost five stone in weight from being unable to eat. John Ogilvie was held to have interceded and so was canonised in 1976, the first Scottish saint since Queen Margaret in 1250. John Fagan, completely better, was at the Vatican to see it happen.

AD 1638-1647

HORRORS OF
THE COVENANT!

IN 1643 THE Kirk Session members were feeling their oats: they went about chastising and fining Glasgow folks for swearing, blaspheming and being 'mockers of piety', and they were particularly hard on 'offenders against the seventh commandment' (Thou shalt not commit adultery). It must have been like the Spanish Inquisition, with every kirk-session meeting inquiring into the private affairs of the citizens, and with elders expected to spy on each other and report misconduct.

However, by this time Scotland was in uproar as Charles I had set in motion the events that would ultimately lead to the Wars of the Three Kingdoms (the English call this the Civil War, as if only England was involved). Charles thought he had a divine right to rule, fancied having the bishops back in charge and imposed a new form of liturgy on the Scots. There were riots, and the Covenant of 1581 was resurrected early in 1638, to be sent all over Scotland for signing.

In 1643, Scottish Royalists (chiefly Roman Catholics and Episcopalians) opposed the Covenanters. This led to civil war in Scotland during the years 1644-47.

James Graham, 1st Marquess of Montrose, had initially been on the Covenanter side, but switched to the Royalist. General David Leslie was in command of the Covenanter army.

Along with Irish mercenaries and Highland clans led by Alasdair MacColla, Montrose initially won his fights against the Covenanters, including the battle of Kilsyth. Montrose was now more or less in command of Scotland, as Lord Lieutenant and Captain-General – almost the King's viceroy. Edinburgh released prisoners to him and Glasgow invited him in. However, Montrose misjudged the mood of his Highlanders when he forbade any looting and plundering while in the city, even hanging a few miscreants who did – thereby taking most of the fun out of being there, from their perspective. All the Gordons went off in a snit. Alasdair MacColl was knighted for his part, but as he was, after all, a MacDonald, he wanted to get back to his real business of fighting with the Campbells back in the west. There was no chance of reinforcements from the Lowlands, so it was a rather bare and sparse army that Montrose led to Philiphaugh, near Selkirk, on 13 September.

GLASGOW MUST PAY!

General David Leslie, of the Covenanter army, was so miffed that the Glasgow citizens had lent Montrose 50,000 merks that he imposed a penalty of £20,000 Scots. Mind you, it didn't stop the remarkable George Porterfield buying the lands of Gorbals and Bridgend from Robert Douglas, Viscount Belhaven, for 140,000 merks in 1648, largely using money from Hutcheson's Hospital and the Trades, who each got some of the land in return. The war, and its cost, meant that Lord Belhaven only got half the money. He was ruined as a consequence.

Covenanter clergy also made Glasgow suffer further for supporting the Marquess of Montrose. Council elections were overturned and Covenanter place-men put in office. The citizens were required to dig a defensive trench around the town at their own expense; they also had an expensive garrison of almost 1,000 men billeted on them (which George Porterfield had to feed). Parliament also made Glasgow pay 3,000 merks to the officers of various regiments and stable their baggage horses – and, as a final indignity, the town had to contribute over £1,530 Scots to the pay of the army which beat Montrose at Philiphaugh. This was at a time when three years of pestilence was already ravaging the city's resources. A merk, by the way, was two-thirds of a Scottish pound.

There they met a bloody end: Montrose was surprised, largely by Covenanter forces returning from England. General David Leslie had quickly marched some 4,000 horses and infantry from Hereford, who were more than a match for the 300 largely Irish troops and cavalry of Montrose – especially as over 1,000 of his men chose to adopt a time-honoured Scottish tactic of sitting out the fighting until the smoke clears then managing to be found standing with the winning side. Of those 300, at least 250 were killed in battle, but the butchery escalated: 300 wives, children, wounded soldiers, other camp-followers and prisoners were cruelly slaughtered – 'like vermin', one commentator put it – in the courtyard of Newark Castle as Leslie's men took revenge for Kilsyth, and a further eighty women and children were thrown into the Avon near Linlithgow, to drown.

Patrick Gordon of Ruthven, writing in *A Short Abridgement of Britane's Distemper* in 1650 about the treatment of Irish mercenaries by the Scots, said:

> It seemed to them there was no distinction betwixt a man and a beast: for they killed men ordinarily with no more feeling of compassion, and with the same careless neglect, that they kill ane henn or capone for ther supper. And they were also without all shame, most brutishlie given to uncleanness and filthie lust.

The 'justice' meted out to the Irish partly arose from the massacres attending the rebellion of 1641-42, in which some of the Irish officers had been involved. The most terrible atrocities were committed by the Irish rebels on Protestants, with children killing other children (and adults), and children hung up on hooks to die; people were spiked on the ends of pointed stakes and the dead thrown to dogs. Some 27,000 persons are reckoned to have been murdered. The Lord President at the trial of Sir Phelim O'Neil, one of the instigators, was right to ask 'was he born of a woman who did this?'

Parliament, bent on vengeance, had ordered all prisoners taken at or after Philiphaugh to be executed 'without any assize or process' and 'without sentence, or the least formality of Law', according to Sir George Mackenzie – Lord Advocate and better known as 'Bluidy MacKenzie' for his robust attitude towards Covenanters. The captured Irish leaders O'Cahan and M'Lachlan were executed in Edinburgh. Sir Robert Spottiswood, the Lord President and son of the archbishop, was tried and executed at St Andrews on 20 January 1646,

along with Nathaniel Gordon and Captain Andrew Guthrie, son of the Bishop of Moray. And three of the ringleaders – Sir William Rollo, Sir Philip Nisbet, and Alexander Ogilvy of Inverquharity (only eighteen years old) – were taken to be beheaded at Glasgow.

Guthrie related that David Dickson, Professor of Divinity in Glasgow University, commented in a rather bloodthirsty way on the executions of the remaining two men: 'The work goes bonnily on'. The minutes of the Committee of Estates make grim reading:

GLASGOW, 21 October 1645
Forsameikle as by decreit and sentence of parliament of the fyft and elevent of Februarie last Mr William Rollock Alexander Ogilvie of Innerquharitie and Sir Philip Nisbet are forfault and doome and sentence of law pronounced against them be a dempster for the causes conteaned in the said sentence as the same read and considered be the lords and others of the committie more full proports. Therefor the said committie ordeanes the said Mr William

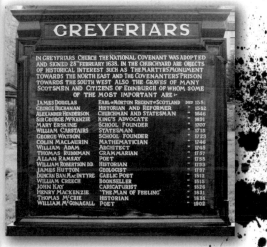

Memorials to the Covenanters, including the prison that held them.

THE CORPSE OF MONTROSE

When news of the executions reached Montrose in the north, he returned to Glasgow with some 1,200 foot and 300 horse, only to find it guarded by Leslie's cavalry of 3,000. For almost a month he harried Glasgow daily, trying to get Leslie out to do battle. Leslie didn't bother, and on the whole treated Glasgow and its citizens rather well. The Great Montrose then made one more push against Leslie, but he was defeated at Carbisdale. He was hanged and beheaded at Edinburgh and his head spiked at the Old Tolbooth, his arms and legs sent to Glasgow, Perth, Stirling and Aberdeen and the rest of his body buried ignominiously on the Burgh Muir.

Eleven years later, in 1661, his corpse was disinterred, reunited with his head and limbs, and he was given a proper lying-in-state at Holyrood with a suitably opulent coffin. A real state funeral was held in Saint Giles's on 11 May, attended by nobles on horseback, thousands of the public on foot, with trumpets blaring, banners flying and cannon firing. Inscribed on his tomb is a poem by Montrose himself:

Scatter my ashes, strew them in the air
Lord, since thou knowest where all these atoms are....

Rollock Alexander Ogilvie and sir Philip Nisbet now prisoners in Glasgow and who wer latly tane in rebellioun with James Graham to be brought befor the comittie presently and the sentence forsaid to be intimat and read to them and given out as doome of law be a dempster. Lykas the saids three trators being personally present before the comittie the said sentence was read in their hearing and the doome therein conteaned pronounced be Johne Wilson dempster. The execution wheroff the committie ordeanes to be upon the person of the said Mr William Rollock this afternoone at the mercat croce of Glasgow and upon the saids Alexander Ogilvie and sir Philip Nisbet at the same place upon the morne afternone by straiking off thair heads from thair bodies, and ordeanes the provost and baillies of Glasgow to sie this sentence put in execution.

It's worth noting that none of the three so-called 'trators' had anything much to do with Glasgow, but were made an example of in a city which had been rather too welcoming to Montrose and his Royalists after the Battle of Kilsyth (15 August 1645), and whose citizens needed to be taught a lesson. Rollo was beheaded at 4 p.m. on 21 October on a large scaffold erected above the Cross; the two other men were beheaded the next morning.

The executions of Rollo and the others were followed by a plague, then a famine, then the great fire of 1652 that destroyed the wooden-fronted houses of the Saltmarket, Trongate and High Street. 'No respite for the wicked', the Glasgow Presbyterians must have thought.

AD 1646

CROMWELL IN GLASGOW

ALTHOUGH CHARLES I surrendered himself to the Scots in 1646, he refused to accept the Covenant. A Scottish army invaded England in support of the 'Engagement' (as it was known) but got beaten at the Battle of Preston. After Charles I was beheaded, Charles II landed in Scotland in June 1650 and swore an oath to approve the Covenants, renewed when he was crowned at Scone the next January.

Cromwell took it badly. He invaded Scotland, defeated the Scots and in 1650-52 occupied it with his New Model Army, utterly sidelining the Covenanters and forcing a union with England. Glasgow had raised troops and arms from a levy of 9,000 merks on the citizens, but it was to no avail. Frankly, if the Church hadn't interfered with the army – expelling experienced officers for not being Protestant enough, for example – Cromwell might well have turned back. As it was, the Campbells of Blythswood had the pleasure of entertaining Cromwell at their Saltmarket mansion, Silvercraigs, when the Protector visited Glasgow.

The Campbells (afterwards of Blythswood) more or less ran Glasgow for

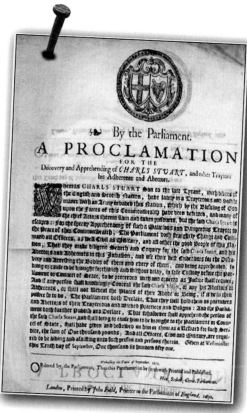

The 'Wanted Poster' for Charles II, in which Cromwell 'offers a reward of reward of £1,000 for the arrest of the son of the late Tyrant'.

a while. Descended from one of the oldest merchant families, they started to amass their wealth during the reign of Mary. Colin Campbell senior was a merchant burgess and a bailie of Glasgow in 1615. His only son, Colin Campbell Junior, was bailie in 1628 and provost in 1636. His eldest son, Robert Campbell of Elie and Silvercraigs, was the one who accommodated Oliver Cromwell in 1650, in their house in the Saltmarket, opposite the Briggaite. His second son, Colin Campbell the third, elder of Blythswood, became provost of Glasgow in 1661, and his brother, James, in 1669, at the same time as another brother, Robert, was dean of the guild.

It is fair to say that General David Leslie – still commanding the Scottish Royalists at this point – had led Cromwell a merry dance for months. But at last he prevailed at Dunbar on 3 September 1650, so Scotland was his for the taking. A letter written at the time told that:

> On Friday afternoon, October 24, 1650, we reached Glasgow. That morning my lord, at a rendezvous, gave a special charge to all the regiments of the army to carry themselves civilly and do no wrong to any. The town of Glasgow, though not so big and rich, yet to all seems a much sweeter and more delightful place than Edinburgh.

How nice. And the Marquis of Argyle had had the good manners to scuttle out of town to make room for him. But the good folks of Glasgow had a warm welcome awaiting Cromwell: they had filled the Bishop's Castle vault with gunpowder, with the idea of blowing him up as he entered from the top of the High Street. Cromwell, getting wind of this, instead rode into the city via Cowcaddens and Cow Loan (now

Queen Street) and took up lodgings in Silvercraigs Land with Campbell.

That Sunday, Cromwell went to the High Church, and Zachary Boyd, the barony's minister, 'opened his mind so freely upon him, that Captain Thurlow, the general's secretary, wanted to pistol him where he stood'. Cromwell had a better way of dealing with the argumentative Boyd: he invited Zach to dinner and made him sit through a prayer that lasted three hours, into the early morning. Boyd had written in *The Sickman's Sore*: 'There was never an age more fertile in reproofs and reproches than this: we are come to the dregges of dayes, where it is counted vertue to point out the imperfections of our brethren. Many are like the Flee that can not rest but upon a Scabbe'.

The Glasgow citizenry were very much in two minds about Cromwell: on the one hand, to fight as Covenanters and Royalists side-by-side for a Covenanted King, 'for Christ and Scotland', as Carlyle puts it; on the other, to stand against the New Model Army, the most potent and disciplined fighting force of its day. There was, Carlyle

The Bishop's Castle, where gunpowder to blow up Cromwell was placed.

THE BLYTHSWOOD BODY

Colin Campbell had purchased the Blythswood estate from the creditors of Sir George Elphinstone. Sir George had organised the erection of the Gorbals into a Burgh of Barony and Regality, but was so poor by the time that he died, in 1634, that his actual body was arrested by creditors, and had to be bought back by his friends for private burial.

He was buried in the chapel next to his home. The last resting place of his corpse was later used as a prison and courthouse, and was an abandoned ruin by the early 1870s.

says, '... some foolish tumult in Glasgow [which] was quelled by the intervention of Cromwell's soldiers'. Anyway, the Lord Protector and his Roundheads left on the Monday to deal with an outbreak of something or other rumoured at Stirling.

He did visit Glasgow again in April 1651, safe enough with Leslie still in the far north. This time, when he went to church, Cromwell heard the minister Robert Ramsay give a sermon that he found to his liking, and offered to host a meeting to debate religious and political matters. The star of this occasion was the Revd Hugh Binning, who had been elected to the chair of philosophy in Glasgow at nineteen years old, and whose 'eloquence, fervour, and great theological attainments' ran rings around Cromwell's Independent clergy. Cromwell asked the name of 'that learned and bold young man' and said: 'He hath bound well indeed, but (putting his hand on his sword) this will loose all again'. Anyway, Binning died of consumption two years later, aged twenty-six.

Cromwell left Glasgow after ten days or so, and came to be called 'Gramaghee', a Gaelic soubriquet signifying someone who holds fast, as in a vice-like grip.

Cromwell's time was probably, on balance, good for Scotland. His military presence at Ayr, Leith, Perth, and Inverness stayed any armed uprisings; Glasgow benefited from the to-ing and fro-ing of troops, with the need for billeting, food, transport and so on; the tyrannical rule of Covenanting ministers was ended; Glasgow had a Commissioner at the Westminster Parliament; the union introduced the stable Commonwealth currency into Scotland and opened up free trade with England and the colonies. The first of the great coal-mines on the south side were opened. Yes, there was some loss of sovereignty, but without this, and the opportunity it gave Glasgow to draw breath, gather its strength and rebuild its economy, it might have stayed essentially a fishing village with a market, a cathedral and a university, rather than the industrial and import-export powerhouse it has become.

THE KILLING TIME

THE COVENANTERS HAD not gone away, and were back in force during the later 1670s. Over the next few years thousands of Presbyterians were persecuted and killed for holding to the Covenanter persuasion.

In 1677, the Government was again firmly in the grip of Charles II, who was a secret Catholic: he had restored Episcopal government to Scotland in 1661 and banned the mainly outdoor preaching sessions called Conventicles. A bond was circulated to which the people of Glasgow were ordered to subscribe, involving total renunciation of Presbyterianism. Many refused, as they equated religious freedom with civic and political liberty. So the Highland Host was again unleashed on the city, made up of 'the very scum of that uncivilised country' – an estimated 10,000 in all. The Celts arrived on 26 June 1678. *History of the Suffering of the Church in Scotland* described their supplies:

> They had no small store of ammunition, four field-pieces, vast numbers of spades, shovels, mattocks, as if they had been to have attacked great fortifications. They had a good store of iron shackles, as if

they were to lead back vast numbers of slaves; and thumb-locks, as they call them, to make their examinations and trials with.

The spades and sacks had been brought for the purpose of plundering Glasgow, and they terrorised the townsfolk while living free for almost a week, quartered on 'recusants' who had refused to sign the Bond.

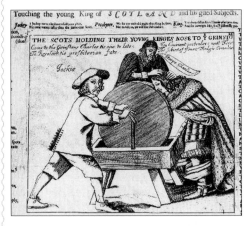

Coventanters in action! Charles II being held with his nose to the grindstone by the Scots in 1651. Sadly, this didn't actually happen, except allegorically.

The Highland hordes were thoroughly given their character by William Cleland, son of the Marquess of Douglas's gamekeeper, but an educated man and a great soldier:

> For truly, they more cruel carrie,
> Than ever Frenchmen under Yarie,
> Or Spaniards under Ferdinando did,
> Or French, when Duke of Guise commanded,
> Yea they more savage far than those were,
> Who with Kollkittoch and Montrose were,
> And sixtie times they're worse than they
> Whom Turner led in Galloway,
> They durk our Tennents, shames our Wives,
> And we're in hazard of our Lives,
> They plunder horse, and them they loaden,
> With Coverings, Blankets, Sheets and Plaidin'
> With Hooding gray, and worsted stuff,
> They sell our Tongs for locks of snuff,
> They take our Cultors and our soaks,
> And from our doors they pull the locks,
> They leave us neither shoals nor spaids,
> And takes away our Iron in laids,
> They break our pleughs, ev'n when they're working
> We dare not hinder them for durking:
> My Lords, they so harasse and wrong us:
> There's scarce a pair of shoes among us,
> And for Blew bonnets they leave non,
> That they can get Clauts upon,
> If any dare refuse to give them,
> They Durk them, strips them, and so leaves them.

Then the 'Red Shanks' headed off for a similar engagement in Ayrshire, where they are said to have netted almost £140,000 Scots. They also fancied a return match in Glasgow, but this time students and other young men barred the bridge, and as the river was high they had to give up their loot. Then 2,000 of them were forced to leave by the West Port in parties of no more than forty. So that was a win in extra time for Glasgow!

Feelings were running high against Covenanters, though. When the great fire of 1677 broke out the council refused to let the prisoners out of the Tolbooth, and most of them were Covenanters. Glaswegians took ladders and set them free, including Kerr of Kersland, who had been imprisoned for eight years there and elsewhere. Unsurprisingly, he took some of the others victims of persecution and headed for Protestant Utrecht, where he died three years later.

TRAMPLED TO DEATH IN THE STREETS OF GLASGOW

But there was yet another rebellion in 1679, when a relatively poorly-armed bunch of Covenanters (yes, they hadn't gone away) took on John Graham of Claverhouse and government forces at the Battle of Drumclog. Graham – later known as 'Bonnie Dundee' or 'Bluidy Clavers', depending on your viewpoint – had started it by attacking a outdoor Conventicle on Loudoun Hill, Ayrshire. On Sunday 1 June, the Revd Thomas Douglas finished his sermon with the rousing phrase, 'Ye have the theory, now for the practice!' Oh yes: they were indeed ready.

Doubtless, Graham thought he would meet a disorganised rabble at Loudon Hill. In fact, the 200-strong Covenanter force was armed with muskets and pitchforks and had some forty mounted men. They were well prepared, ably commanded by Robert Hamilton, and they had a plan. Moving to a boggy moor – or 'stank', in the local parlance – on Drumclog farm, they were in a position where Graham's men found it impossible to engage them because of the ground conditions, which bogged them down at every attack. When the Covenanters decided to press their advantage, they skirted the bog and advanced, despite heavy fire from the government dragoons. Graham's line broke and was routed, leaving thirty-six dead.

On their way out to Drumclog, the government cavalry had ridden so hard through the Glasgow streets that one of them had trampled and killed a child. When Graham had to retreat and slink back to Glasgow, defeated, the city folk felt it was no more than he deserved.

CORPSES IN THE STREETS!

The Covenanters followed up their triumph at Drumclog by attacking Glasgow a few days later, now defended by a small force of soldiers under Claverhouse and Lord Ross. By contrast, the numbers of the rebels had swelled, and they marched into the city in two columns – one by the Gallowgait and the other by the College Lands and Wyndhead. They were met by Royalist troops dug in behind barricades at Glasgow Cross and the Tolbooth, and by virtue of discipline, training and superior firepower from Claverhouse the insurgents found themselves beaten back – with eight deaths, and many casualties. Living up to his 'Bluidy' epithet, Clavers refused to allow the citizens to take away the bodies, which lay in the streets until the Covenanters, with even more reinforcements, again marched on the city. In this instance the Royalists decided discretion was the better part of everything and scuttled to Kilsyth – traditionally, fierce Covenanting country.

BOTHWELL BRIDGE

Sadly for the rebels, their hopes were dashed on 22 June at the battle of Bothwell Bridge. More and more people, sick of the persecution of Covenanting, flocked to join a rebel camp at Bothwell, near Glasgow, but three weeks later the Battle of Bothwell Brig ended badly for them.

The Covenanters spent the next few weeks rebuilding their numbers to around 6,000. King Charles' eldest illegitimate son James, Duke of Monmouth (later 1st Duke of Buccleuch), was dispatched to take command of the King's 5,000 troops, with Claverhouse under him.

The rebels had set up camp just north of Hamilton and on the south bank of the Clyde. Robert Hamilton was nominally in command, but wasn't there. Fortunately, there were other competent leaders. These included Donald Cargill, once the minister of the barony parish (successor to the eminent Zachary Boyd, but ejected in 1662 for rhetorically 'rebuking' King Charles), and William Cleland, who fought so ably at Drumclog. Monmouth had to force his way across the narrow Bothwell Bridge to get at the Covenanters, who defended it for an hour until their ammunition ran out. Once across, Monmouth's troops skirmished and routed the Covenanters, many of whom took refuge in the grounds of Hamilton Palace: Anne, Duchess of Hamilton, was sympathetic to the Presbyterians.

However, some 600 men were killed and perhaps 1,400 more were taken as captives to Edinburgh, where they were confined for months without shelter in Greyfriars' Kirkyard. Some died, some were executed for treason, a few escaped and others signed a pledge of loyalty to the Crown for their freedom. But the remaining 257 were transported to

HORRIBLE HIGHLANDERS!

The Highland host were colourfully described by an eye-witness a few months before they reached Glasgow:

> You know the fashion of the wild apparel, not one of them hath breeches, yet hose and shoes are their greatest need and clever prey; and they spare not to take them [steal them] every where… As for their armes and other militarie accoutrements, it is not possible for me to describe them in writing; here you may see head-pieces and steel-bonnets raised like pyramids, and such as a man would affirme they had only found in chamber-boxes; targets and shields of the most odde and antique forme, and powder horns hung with strings, garnished with beaten nails and burnished brass. And I truly doubt not but that a man, curious of our antiquities, might in this host finde explications of the strange pieces of armour mentioned in our old lawes, such as the bosnet, iron, hat, gorget, pesane, wambrassers, and reerbrassers, pans, leg-splents, and the like, above what any occasion in the Lowlands would have afforded for several hundreds of yeers.

Ten years later, a visitor to Mull described the locals:

> I generally observed the men to be large-bodied, stout, subtle, active, patient of cold and hunger… Their thighs are bare, with brawny muscles… What should be concealed is hid with a large shot pouch, on each side of which hangs a pistol and a dagger, as if they found it well necessary to keep those parts well guarded. A round target [shield] on their back, a blew bonnet on their head, in one hand a broadsword and a musquet in the other. Perhaps no nation goes better armed; and I assure you they will handle them with bravery and dexterity.

In 1726, an English officer had this to say about Highland dress: 'Some I have seen shod with a kind of pumps made out of a raw cow hide with the hair turned outwards… [These are] not only offensive to the sight, but intolerable to the smell of those near them.' The officer also warned of the skeen-occles, a sharp dagger nearly a foot long hidden by the armpit, 'a concealed mischief under the plaid, ready for the secret stabbing, and in a close encounter there is no defence against it.'

---

the colonies, only to be shipwrecked when their ship, the *Crown of London*, went down at Scarvataing, Orkney, on 10 December 1679. Locked in the hold, 210 men drowned. The forty or so prisoners who survived were recaptured and sent to Jamaica or New Jersey. A Covenanters' Monument was erected at nearby Deerness in 1888 and there is a corresponding memorial in Greyfriars, unveiled in 2007.

PAPISTS IN GLASGOW

Whilst all of this was going on, Glasgow entertained King James right royally and sent him wine 'of the grouth 1680' – presumably a good year. The entire council and body of magistrates waited on him, the young men of the town made a bodyguard and it was proclaimed that all citizens should light bonfires at the head of their closes when they heard the Toun Bell ringing at Albany's approach.

He was made a burgess, and when he dined at Provost Bell's house in the Briggait, the whole exercise cost over £4,000 in Scottish money, what with food, wine, sweetmeats, the gilt and silver boxes in which burgess tickets were presented to Albany and his retinue and drinks for his servants. Bell received a knighthood as a thank you. In fact, Scotland rather took to James: he encouraged Scottish manufacturers; he played golf and tennis with the aristocracy, and his wife, Mary of Este, charmed their ladies by introducing them to the brand-new fashion of drinking tea. The only sour note was James having a protest against the 'persecutions' handed to him as he left Glasgow.

Not everyone had a good time, though. John Spreull, an apothecary, whose father was being hunted by the authorities, was apprehended, tried and released, fleeing the country in fear for his continued safety. His wife and family were dispossessed and Spreull's house, shop and goods seized. When he came back, about the time of the Battle of Bothwell Bridge, he really meant to collect his wife and children to return with him to Rotterdam. However, he was captured and put to the question: did he know anything about the murder of Archbishop James Sharp, King Charles's enforcer in Scotland, who had been assassinated by a band of nine Covenanters on Magus Muir, outside St Andrews, on 3 May? (The men were actually lying in wait for the Sheriff of Cupar, but seeing Sharp's coach they thought: 'He'll do!' and stabbed Sharp multiple times in front of his daughter.) Did he know anything about the Drumclog and Bothwell rebellions?

They used 'the boot', hammering the wedges ever tighter as he denied any knowledge of these affairs – or of a plot to blow up the Duke of Albany, or the wherea-

bouts of Donald Cargill. This was so ineffective that they brought a new boot and Spreull was tortured all over again. His feet were so destroyed that he had to be carried to prison on a soldier's back, but he refused the attentions of a surgeon. He was, of course, found guilty (absence of actual proof was never an issue), was fined £500 sterling and imprisoned on the Bass Rock for almost six years – accounting for the name the citizens afterwards knew him by, 'Bass John'.

THREE MURDERED COVENANTERS

Cathcart old parish church graveyard has the grave of three Covenanters – Robert Thome, Thomas Cooke and John Urie – murdered in 1685. On the top is written:

This is the stone tomb of Robert Thome, Thomas Cooke and John Urie, martyrs for ounng the covenanted work of Reformation on 11 of May 1685. The bloody murderers of these men were Magor Balfour and Captain Metland ... as soon as they had them out found they murthered them with shots of guns. Scarce time did they to them allow befor ther maker ther knies to bow many like in this land have been whos blood for wingance crys to heavn this cruell wickedness you see was don in lon of Polmadie. This may a standing witness be `twixt prisbytrie and prelacie.

Many Covenanters were transported for their pains – held at Dunottar Castle before being shipped off from Leith. However, they had the option of taking an oath of allegiance and two Glasgow men, John Marshall and David Fergusson, did so and were freed. The rest went to New Jersey, which is punishment enough.

BRING ME THE HEAD OF RICHARD CAMERON!

As the strife wore on, the English authorized field executions without trial – the period afterwards known as the 'Killing Time'. Daniel Defoe estimated some 18,000 were killed in the period 1661-1680. Many of these were the 'Cameronians', followers of an extreme Coventanting sect led by Revd Richard Cameron.

Glasgow had its own Cameronian martyrs, executed in October 1684: James Lawson and Alexander Wood. At a trial presided over by the William Douglas, Duke of Hamilton, and defended by Lord Ross and a troop of dragoons, both men gave an eloquent testimony. They had heard both Richard Cameron and Donald Cargill – the minister at Glasgow Barony Parish, who once gave a sermon in which he excommunicated Kings Charles and James and delivered them up to Satan 'with several other rotten malignant enemies' – preach in 1680 to 1681.

The execution was at the Howgate, then just outside the burgh and used for the purpose until the 1780s. Their joint testimony says:

> ... we leave our testimony against these wicked men called judges, which ought not to be called judges, but rather tyrants, because they are thirsting for blood; for they charge us in one of the articles of our indictment with murder, and shaking off all the fear of God; but we bless the Lord we are free of all such crimes as murder.... Now, we bid farewell to all earthly comforts and enjoyments.... Farewell sweet prison and irons for our lovely Lord.... Farewell sun, moon, and stars, and all created comforts in time...

Crowds at Cameron's services grew as he went around the south west of Scotland, and he gave what was to be his last sermon at Kype Water, near Styrathaven, south-east of Glasgow. He told the congregation:

> ... our Lord is to set up a standard, and oh that it may be carried to Scotland! When it is set up, it shall be carried through the nations; and it shall go to Rome, and the gates of Rome shall be burnt with fire. It is a standard that shall overthrow the throne of Britain, and all the thrones in Europe...

On 22 July, with around sixty followers on horse and foot, Cameron was set upon by government dragoons led by Andrew

The grave slab of Richard Cameron and eight other Covenanters at Airds Moss. They were killed in the battle here on 22 July 1680. (© Walter Baxter)

THE MAIDEN

In 1685, Archibald Campbell, 9th Earl of Argyll and Chief of Clan Campbell, launched a rebellion using money borrowed by his father from Hutchesons' Hospital and Glasgow Council. He marched on Glasgow, but managed to leave most of his provisions and ammunition on an island in the Kyles of Bute and get his army lost in the bogs of the Kilpatrick Hills while trying to sneak into Glasgow by the back door.

Many of the Highlanders just got fed up and headed north for home. His force dispersed, Argyll crossed the Clyde, changed clothes with a peasant he met and skulked away, only to be caught. He spent the night in Glasgow Tolbooth before being sent to Edinburgh for execution on the Maiden on 30 June. (Argyll's son, Archibald Campbell, 9th Earl of Argyll, was also executed on the Maiden in 1685, for leading a rebellion against James VII.) Revd James Guthrie, minister at Stirling, was the second person to be executed and is said to have lifted the handkerchief covering his face and shouted, 'The Covenant, the Covenant, shall yet be Scotland's reviving!'

It seems that the Maiden was introduced to Scotland by James Douglas, 4th Earl of Morton, while Regent to the young James VI. He had seen it used in Halifax, and had a model made to bring home; a full-scale version was built in 1564. The name 'Maiden' was applied to it because it was largely unused after Thomas Scott of Cambusmichael became its first victim in 1565 – until Morton himself felt its embrace in 1581.

The mechanism was a sort of weighted blade which ran in grooves in the frame. The condemned was placed with head on the crossbar, and a cord pulled to detach a peg, releasing the weights, causing the blade to fall and thus decapitating the guilty party. In a particularly humorous twist, if the crime had been, say, stealing a horse, the steed concerned was tied to the rope and whipped: stung, it would pull out the peg and was, technically, the executioner.

Before it was taken away in 1708, the Maiden claimed over 150 lives. It can still be seen at the National Museum of Scotland.

*The Covenant
is reviving!*

Bruce of Earlshall ('Bluidy Bruce'), who tracked him down at Airds Moss. Cameron's 'Hill Men' were outnumbered but, as Bruce later reported, 'The dispute continued a quarter of an hour very hot; the rebels, refusing either to fly or take quarter, fought like madmen.'

Cameron was killed. His head and hands were severed from his body and taken to Edinburgh, where they were shown to his father, who was held in the Tolbooth. His head was then paraded up the street on a pole, and set up for public display at the Netherbow.

Many of Cameron's 'Hill Men' were hanged at Glasgow, their heads put up on pikes at the gaol, and their bodies buried on the north side of the cathedral church. A stone erected later to the Glasgow Martyrs says:

These nine, with others in this yard
Whose heads and bodies were not spared,
Their testimonies foes to bury,
Cans'd beat the drums then in great fury,
They'll know at resurrection day,
To murder saints was no sweet play.

The Cameronians ultimately became the (26th) Scottish Rifles Regiment of that name, disbanded in 1968.

WITCHES EVERYWHERE

WHEN **KING JAMES** VI of Scotland became James I of England in 1603, he was known as 'Scotch Jimmy', although it's unknown whether he ever wore the comical hat. He led the way in many things, not least a hate campaign which was to find Glasgow gripped in mortal terror for decades: the witch persecutions.

James was a rather scarred young man – he never got to know his mother, had been brought up to rule from infancy and was forever having to balance the various 'advisors' who had their own agendas. James did not inherit Mary's renowned beauty; he was squat and ungainly, with crooked legs, and he was moody, conceited, boorish, cowardly, slobbered from an over-large tongue and shouted a lot. He was also rendered rather joyless by the necessary Calvinism, but he could swear like a trooper and take part in drunken revelries. On the other hand, he was well-read and scholarly ('the wisest fool in Christendom').

All of this combined to produce in him what was probably a sadistic love of torment, which found its expression in his pursuit of practitioners of second sight, folk-healing and witchcraft. He enjoyed (not too strong a word for it) watching elderly women persecuted and tortured for suspected possession and for practicing the Black Arts, although he never could understand why the Devil seemed to prefer aged crones to buxom young wenches – which James himself certainly did.

This had all started in the 1590s, just after James's marriage to Anne of Denmark, sister of King Christian IV. On the return to Scotland of the happy couple, violent storms led to them seeking shelter in Norway for a few weeks. The Danish admiral commanding the escort blamed the whole thing on the wife of an official in Copenhagen, a known witch, whom he, the admiral, had insulted. James took this seriously and even implicated several of the Scottish nobles.

There were witchcraft trials in both Denmark and Scotland, the best known of which were of the North Berwick 'witches'. They confessed (when tortured, of course) to meeting the Devil in a church at night, attempting to poison the King and his friends, and sending the bad weather to sink the King's ship. Agnes Sampson was personally examined by James VI at

Holyrood, where she was fastened to a cell wall by a witch's bridle. This iron device, a development of the 'scold's bridle' or 'branks' used to punish gossiping, slander and blasphemy, had four sharp prongs that pressed into the tongue and cheeks. After that – plus the usual sleep-deprivation and having her head squeezed by a rope – Agnes naturally confessed to over fifty charges, proving that her accusers were right all along. She was then strangled and burned.

There were five main witch-hunt episodes in Scotland: 1590-1591; 1597; 1628-1631; 1649; and 1661-1662. The two main outbreaks of witch fever in Glasgow were one in the 1620s and another at the end of the century. It is probably not a coincidence that the first happened when James had briefly restored the Episcopacy, so that the various clerical and secular authorities were falling over themselves to try, torture and burn anyone suspected of 'heresy' – which really meant anything they didn't approve of, and so much the better if it could be dressed up as witchcraft.

Quite possibly, 3,000 to 4,000 Scots were executed as witches between 1560 and 1707, according to historian T.C. Smout. Even if that is an over-estimate, there are surviving records of almost 2,000 witchcraft trials. Glasgow more or less escaped the epidemic of witch trials and executions, although places nearby were infected. The most famous trials were the 'bewitching' of Sir George Maxwell of Pollok in 1677-78 and, in the 1696-97, the celebrated case of Christian Shaw at Bargarran, near Erskine Ferry, after which three men and four women were accused: one committed suicide in prison, and the other six were burned at the stake on Paisley Green.

In Glasgow, the main victims of witch-hysteria were Christiane Grahame, in

The North Berwick witches.

1621; Catherine Blair and Margaret Wallace in 1622; and Grissell Boill, Janet Miller and Jean Miller in 1629. Christiane Grahame was accused of what we would now call folk-healing. She was named by another witch, and executed. Margaret Wallace was caught up in a neighbourhood quarrel and a business dispute her husband was having with fellow-craftsmen, but she was also accused of murdering Mr Archibald Glen, minister at Carmunnock, in 1614. He had been investigating whether she was practicing witchcraft at the time.

The next epidemic of Satanic panic, in 1699-1700, caught the following unfortunates: Jean Greenlaw; Mary McKinnie; a lady known only by her surname, Bell; plus Margaret Duncan, Jannet Gentleman and Marion Ure.

Margaret Duncan, whose trial lasted from April 1699 to March 1700, was accused of demonic possession. Margaret was a widow whose husband, John Bell, had been a merchant. She is described as having tormented Margaret Murdoch (in Govan) and Margaret Laird (in Paisley) – a charge also levelled at Agnes Supp of Port Glasgow, whose employer fired her from her position as servant for her alleged witchcraft. The two Margarets also named Margaret Duncan and Jannet Gentleman, as well as one Mistress Bell, Jean Greenlaw and Mary McKinnie, none of whom seem to have been brought to trial.

Marion Ure's late husband had also been a merchant, by the name of George Rae, and Jannet Gentleman was married to George Craighead, described as 'late Beadle'. Outwardly respectable, you might think. This case hinged on the women concerned being denounced by the two girls, Murdoch and Laird. Both claimed to be tormented by witches and pointed the finger at a number of people while in the grip of ecstatic fits. Those who witnessed the fits and accusations also gave testimony. These 'witnesses' were heard in Paisley (19-21 April 1699 from Margaret Laird) and Glasgow (22 April 1699 from Margaret Murdoch).

So what had the three 'witches' been up to? Both Margarets showed all the signs of demonic possession, referred to as 'tormenting' in the trial reports. They had convulsions; they had superhuman strength when so possessed and went in for a great deal of thrashing about; their clothes fell off; they spat up and vomited objects such as pins and stones, but also wool and hair; they showed 'bite and nip markes', as well as bruises and blisters on their bodies and faces; and they had the uncanny ability to sense when their tormenters were nearby. The doctors and ministers attending them were terribly persuaded by all this.

Margaret Duncan, Marion Ure and Jannet Gentleman also appeared to a man in his bedchamber, but quite how he recog-

nised them is a moot point as they appeared as a sow, an ape and a cat.

Jannet Gentleman's husband put up a bond of caution for her – essentially a guarantee of good behaviour backed by a surety of money. So that's all right, then.

Much of the blame for these later cases might be laid at the feet of the minister of Kilmacolm, Revd Dr Brisbane, and his opposite number in Paisley, Mr Thomas Blackwell. Dr William Metcalfe, writing in his *History of the County of Renfrew from the Earliest Times* (1905), sums it up nicely:

> On June 22, 1698, Mr Brisbane, who has so successfully dealt with the 'diabolical' vagaries of his parishioner, Janet Wodrow, intimated that he had discovered a fresh case of the power of Satan in the person of Margaret Laird, who belonged to his own parish of Kilmacolm. Then ensued the usual fasts and prayers, consultations with the Privy Council, letters to the King's advocate, delations, and imprisonments, in all of which Mr. Thomas Blackwell took a prominent part; but, before anything effectual could be done, Mr Blackwell was translated to Aberdeen, where he subsequently became a Professor in the University. His departure wears much the appearance of being the signal for the withdrawal of the forces of Satan from within the county. For, strange to say, shortly after he had gone, the Satanic manifestations against which he had fought so valiantly, began to cease, and the prosecution of witches and the search for them came to an end.

AD 1600-1850

RIOTS, FIRES AND FLOODS

FIRES

The year 1600 was quite a year:

- Scotland celebrated New Year on 1 January for the first time – before that it had been on 25 March, and remained so in England and elsewhere until 1752, which is where the Scots get their reputation for Hogmanay.
- Charles (who would become King Charles I) was born in Dunfermline on 19 November, and would have died had not a skilled healer called Margaret Durie saved the infant – on behalf of the whole Durie family, sorry about that.
- A fire destroyed a third of Glasgow.

This may have been quite a good thing, as it swept away a lot of the cramped, insanitary wooden slums that had harboured the plagues in 1574 and 1584. Unfortunately, however, the Glaswegians just built new slums in their place.

Of course, there were further epidemics in 1645-48, so time for another decent fire. In 1652, one obliged. It started at James Hamilton's house near the Cross and quickly spread along the main roads of Saltmarket, Briggate and Gallowgate. This fire ravaged more than eighty of Glasgow's closes and left over 1,000 families homeless, and – the ultimate indignity – a new-fangled fire engine had to be sent from Edinburgh. (It's OK, though; sculptor James Colquhoun invented one just for Glasgow in 1656 and charged £25 sterling for it.)

But where did the rebuilding money come from? After all, the war had severely depleted the town's resources and this disaster might have ended forever the burgh struggling to become more than a Clydeside village. So, the Town Council swallowed its pride and sent the provost to Ayr, where Cromwell's military government was headquartered, with letters to Edinburgh and the English Parliament. The proceeds of sequestrated estates in Scotland were used to provide £1,000 sterling. The General Assembly ordered a special collection in every church in Scotland. Other burghs like Leith and Aberdeen chipped in.

They rebuilt it well this time, with straight lines and no overhanging 'windskews or hallens', plus four new wells dug, to the extent that Daniel Defoe wrote that the four principal streets were:

... the fairest for breadth and the finest built that I have ever seen... 'tis the cleanest, most beautiful and best built city in Great Britain.... The lower storeys, for the most part, stand on vast Doric columns with arches which open into the shops – adding to the strength as well as to the beauty of the buildings.

But there was yet another fire in 1677, this one started out of pure malice. On 2 November, an apprentice smith, who had been beaten by his master, set fire to the shop. Unfortunately, the fire grew to consume 130 houses and shops, especially in the Saltmarket, and put over 600 families out on the street. The fire reached the Tolbooth and gave an anti-government mob the excuse they needed to break in and free the prisoners. And that was the end of wooden house building.

In 1688, William III, the Prince of Orange, landed in England, and took the English throne. Glasgow went William-crazy. On 30 November of that year, the young Earl of Loudoun and his fellow students at the university decided to celebrate. They burned effigies of the Pope and of the Archbishops of St Andrews and Glasgow. Mobs attacked the Episcopal clergy. Their houses were ransacked, and their wives and children were forced out onto the streets. Even the cathedral was assailed, with a rabble assaulting the magistrates and congregation.

The next major fire started as a result of a drunken spree. One night in February 1793, the Glasgow Hellfire Club (sounds Satanic, but they were just a drinking club, really) got into St Mary's church at the Tron. They built a fire to warm themselves, which inspired them to boast about how they could withstand the fires of Hell – and they built up the fire to prove it. Predictably, it spilled over and set the church ablaze.

The Steeple, built in 1637, was the only surviving part, but it was rebuilt by James Adam the following year as an arch over the pavement. It is now the Tron Theatre, bar and restaurant.

That was more or less it for large-scale fires, but three smaller outbreaks and a false-alarm panic are responsible for Glasgow having three Theatre Royals. This next part is a bit confusing. The Prince's Theatre Royal, Dunlop Street, was opened in January 1782. The owner, John Jackson, later took over the new Theatre Royal in Queen Street in 1805, then the largest in Scotland, which in September 1818 became the first theatre in Britain to be lit by 'Sparkling Gas' instead of oil lamps and candles. The Dunlop Street theatre was renamed the Caledonian. Someone else leased the basement of the Caledonian and started putting on plays in a sort of 'theatre wars' until Glasgow Council told them to behave and show plays on alternate nights. Then the Queen Street theatre was destroyed by fire in 1829, after a rehearsal, so the whole lot moved to the rebuilt Theatre Royal, Dunlop Street.

In 1849 there was a false alarm about a fire in the theatre, and in the panic sixty-five people, mostly apprentice boys, were trampled to death on the stairs. The editor of the Citizen later described the night:

On that terrible evening, Mr Alexander [the owner] was in the midst of the frantic crowd, who were rushing headlong to destruction. He knew that the alarm of fire that had been raised was a false one. He roared himself hoarse in efforts to subdue the panic. A multitude of lives were saved by his vast personal exertions. But the appalling extent of the catastrophe, when revealed, struck heavily at his heart. The pride he was wont to feel in his magnificent theatre was crest-fallen.

He manifested, ever afterwards, an almost superstitious reluctance to go near the fatal staircase.

However, this theatre burnt down for real in 1863. Although rebuilt that year, it was demolished six years later in favour of St Enoch's station. The name was given to The Theatre Royal, Hope Street – which is still there and is apparently fire-proof, touch wood...

FLOODS

Glasgow sits at the confluence of three rivers – Molendinar, Kelvin and Clyde – and it didn't take much for the lower parts of the city to find itself submerged in water. This was eventually solved by deepening the channels in the Clyde, but until then there were several major floods:

- In 1712, those living and working in the Saltmarket and Briggate had to be rescued in boats.
- In 1746, the Laigh Green was under water.
- In 1782, the river rose so high – 20ft, it was said – that at the eastern end of Briggate it was 9ft deep. The Gorbals became an island, and in the town centre victuals were brought in by boat. This is still the greatest flood of the Clyde on record.
- In 1795, yet another flood carried away the nearly-finished bridge being built from the Saltmarket, also taking away the breastwork on the bank. The house of David Dale – the entrepreneur and philanthropist of New Lanark – was so flooded that dinner guests had to be fed from the kitchens of houses next door, and wine had to

Steamers on the Clyde, a river prone to flooding.

be brought from the swamped cellar by Dale's daughter, carried piggy-back by a porter. The evening was a great success, by all accounts. A wooden footbridge was erected over the Clyde, but not until 1804.

- In 1808, the flood ran 'like a mill-race', according to one account, and a man who thought he might try out his boat on Glasgow Green drowned as a consequence.
- In 1816, the Clyde rose 17ft, and Glasgow Green was again under water.
- In 1831, the Clyde inundated the house of William Reid, a bookseller's assistant. This wouldn't matter much (except, possibly, to Mr Reid), except that when young he had been a regular correspondent with Robert Burns and had entertained the poet in Glasgow. All of these valuable records were lost. Reid may even have been the man who dissuaded Burns from emigrating to Jamaica in 1786.

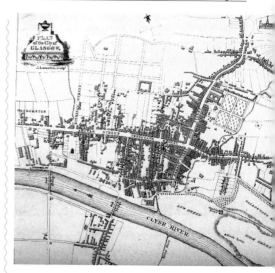

A map of Glasgow in 1783, the year after the greatest flood of the Clyde on record.

OTHER DISASTERS

Glasgow isn't a place much associated with earthquakes, but on 11 August 1786 it did feel the after-shocks of one that spread across the North of England and Western Scotland. There was another on 6 January 1787, but this was localised to Campsie, some 10 miles north. The next one recorded was on 9 November 1852, when a quake of 5.3 Richter, with its epicentre at Caernarfon, was felt in Glasgow.

Most of the city's disasters were man-made. On 15 March 1851 the Victoria coal pit at Nitshill suffered an explosion so loud that it was heard at Paisley. The mine, owned by weavers Coats of Paisley, was the deepest in Scotland at the time. Whatever caused the disaster – gas is blamed, as the miners did not have the Davy safety lamp that would have given them warning – fifty-five men and eight boys were lost. The only saving grace was the time: if it had occurred half an hour later, when the shifts changed, it would have claimed nearer 140 lives. That day and the next, an estimated 20,000 people – principally women and children – assembled at the site. They had all lost fathers, sons, brothers, husbands and friends. It was the greatest death toll in mining up to that date, and led directly to Parliament setting up a select committee on coal mining which produced recommendations about safer working conditions.

YE JACOBITES BY NAME

OLD PRETENDER

These were heady times. Queen Anne, last of the Stuarts, was clearly in her last days and without an obvious heir. The Navigation Laws prevented Scotland trading with 'English' colonies (such as America). Scotland had lost a huge proportion of its capital funds in the disastrous scheme to set up a colony in Darien. And moves were afoot for Union with England.

Glasgow had been looking forward to the events leading up to the Union in 1707 from two different perspectives. Some merchants saw the advantages of being allowed to trade with English colonies in America and the Indies. Others saw profit in the war to come and started laying up gunpowder and other munitions. Almost everybody chose to riot, in one cause or the other.

Glasgow's citizens rejected the 1706 proposal of Union on 7 November – stirred up, as ever, by a firebrand preacher, Revd James Clark, minister of the Tron Kirk, who ended his sermon with the words, 'Wherefore, up and be valiant for the city of our God!' – and burned the Articles of Union at the Cross. The next day, the mob – led by the deacons of the fourteen incorporated trades, no less – assailed the Tolbooth, broke into the provost's house by smashing through his windows, and seized as many

PAPER FOR THE OLD PRETENDER

In 1685, 50,000 French Protestant refugees arrived in Scotland, fleeing persecution by the Sun King, Louis XIV. Many ended up in Glasgow and one of them, Nicholas Desham, started the paper-making industry in Glasgow by picking up rags in the streets and opening a paper mill in Cathcart.

muskets as they could. The provost, unsurprisingly, legged it to Edinburgh. When he came back he discovered an angry crowd waiting for him:

> The rabble immediately gathered around him, thrusting and abusing him, and not with villainous language only, but with stones and dirt and such like thrown at him. He would have made to his own house, but the multitude increasing, and growing furious, he took sanctuary in a house, and running up a staircase lost the rabble for some time – they pursuing him into a wrong house; however, they searched every apartment at the top of the stair, and came into the very room where he was... It is the opinion of many of the soberest and most judicious of citizens, that if they had found him, their fury was at that time so past all government, that they would have murdered him, and that in a manner barbarous enough...

He was forced to hide in a fold-away bed until they had left.

An ex-soldier called Finlay set up his own guard in the ruins of the old Glasgow Castle, and with forty-five other brave souls marched off to Edinburgh to overthrow the Union. Some chance. He failed to meet expected support and slunk back to Glasgow, having missed all the fun of a good-going riot in his absence. Covenanters (yes, they were still around) marched on Dumfries until it finally dawned on them that they were being manipulated by – horror of horrors – Catholics! As it happened, the Union was good for Glasgow's trade, its various growing industries and its intellectual life. But there was more trouble brewing.

On 1 August 1714, Queen Anne died. If her half-brother James (the 'Old Pretender') had been a bit quicker on his feet and willing to espouse the Protestant faith he might have taken the throne: although the Scottish and English Parliaments were united, there were still, in theory, two crowns. But he was not, and his second cousin, George, Elector of Hanover, was proclaimed King in Scotland on 4 August. He landed at Greenwich the next month to start his new job.

In Glasgow a Presbyterian mob headed for a church where the English liturgy was used, and destroyed it. Jacobites were doing much the same in England. John Erskine, 6th Earl of Mar, miffed that he lost his job as Secretary of State for Scotland in favour of the Duke of Montrose, smuggled himself into Scotland on a coal barge and called the Highland chiefs to Braemar on the pretext of hunting, but actually to plan a rebellion. Glasgow's city fathers and Member of Parliament were busy toadying up to the Hanoverians while Mar raised James's standard in the north and a regiment of some 700 Glasgow men and officers, under Colonel Blackadder, was sent from Glasgow to Stirling. Fencibles and militia were raised, trenches dug and barricades erected, cannon were prepared, all to protect Glasgow itself from the expected onrush of Highlanders. A boat commanded by a Highlander called MacDonald was found to be taking on armaments at the Broomielaw quay to be shipped to the Highland Jacobites. However, the Jacobite army was halted at Sheriffmuir on Sunday 13 November – an action that didn't involve Blackadder's Glasgow contingent as they were busy watching Stirling Bridge – and later crushed at Preston, and the rebellion came to nothing.

James Francis Edward, Prince of Wales, the 'Old Pretender', turned up at Peterhead, too late and seasick, and almost immediately turned tail back to France, and the whole uprising left Glasgow with not much more than a financial headache. This it treated by cementing its foothold on the mouth of the Clyde at Port Glasgow, grabbing the tobacco trade, ignoring ministers, cleaning up the town a bit (banning middens was a good start), building itself nice big mansions and starting a newspaper.

What could possibly go wrong? Well, a couple of really good riots, for one thing, but chiefly Prince Charles Edward Louis John Casimir Sylvester Severino Maria Stuart, the Young Pretender – or 'Bonnie Prince Charlie'.

THE YOUNG PRETENDER

Bonnie Prince Charlie also raised an army, and attempted to seize the English throne. On 14 September 1745, Prince Charles and his army stayed a mere 20 miles away from Glasgow. Charles sent a letter to the provost and magistrates demanding – in a very polite way, with lots of promises – £15,000 and 'whatever arms can be found in your city'. That was something like five years' income to Glasgow. Panic ensued – the citizens hid their goods and many fled the town, expecting the Jacobites at

Clementina Walkinshaw by Allan Ramsay.

There is a tradition that Charles left more than a bad impression on Glasgow: the Revd James Stewart, later a minister in Anderston, was widely believed to be Charles's natural son. In April 1746, James' army was routed at Culloden by Prince William, the Duke of Cumberland – known to history as 'Butcher' Cumberland. Glasgow threw a cake-and-wine party to celebrate the Jacobites' defeat and offered the Butcher the freedom of the city.

It's unclear whether the manifold events of 1745 were indeed due to Jacobite versus anti-Jacobite sentiment, or whether they were due to Mr Tennent opening his brewery in the city that year....

What it did do, though, was free up Walkinshaw's Camlachie House for the colonel commanding the regiment which was occupying Glasgow in 1749-50 – later General Wolfe, the cliff-climbing hero of Quebec.

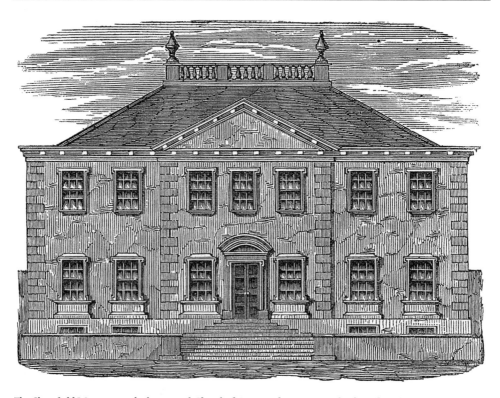

The Shawfield Mansion at the bottom of Glassford Street, where Prince Charles Edward Stuart stayed over Christmas and New Year of 1745-46 and where he is said to have met Clementina Walkinshaw. The house, built by Daniel Campbell in 1711, was the scene of a riot in 1725, as Glaswegians blamed Campbell (MP for the Clyde burghs at the time) for Parliament levying a 2d tax on Scottish malt. Campbell fled Glasgow with his family and valuables on 24 June, and the locals had a fine time ransacking the place. The next day, soldiers sent to the city to keep the peace killed several citizens.

any time. The only defensive force was about thirty Royal Scots Fusiliers, who were away at Dumbarton Castle. Had Charles entered Glasgow, he could have taken it without firing a single shot.

Step forward the rather shrewd Provost Andrew Cochrane, who called a meeting, and sent four men to negotiate with Charles. They got him to lower his demands to £5,500. A private individual, the Earl of Glencairn, lent Glasgow £1,500 towards the loan. This was successful in saving the city, and Cotton Street was renamed Cochrane Street in his honour by a grateful city. Parliament eventually paid back Glasgow £10,000 for what Charles Edward Stuart had taken.

Charles's rag-tag army actually entered Glasgow on Christmas Day, after their retreat from Derby. Tradition goes that they were told to behave themselves, which they did, failing to ransack their billets or abuse their hosts. Charles himself stayed with Colonel William McDowall, the West India sugar baron, in his 'great and stately lodging, orchard, and gardens ... on the north side of the Trongate' – his swanky new mansion house, called Shawfield.

It was also in Glasgow that Bonnie Prince Charlie met his mistress, the Jacobite (and

Catholic convert) Clementina Walkinshaw, by whom he had a daughter, Charlotte. Was that last bit a surprise? Clementina was, as it happens, his mother's god-daughter, and with the same name. He did meet her again, and later she joined him during his exile – but not happily.

Clementina Walkinshaw (1720–1802), who was mistress to the Prince from 1752 until 1760, was the youngest of the ten daughters born to John Walkinshaw, owner of lands of Barrowfield and Camlachie, a wealthy Glasgow merchant (he founded the weaving village of Calton) and an Episcopalian Jacobite. He had fought for the Old Pretender in the 1715 rebellion and was captured at Sheriffmuir, but escaped from Stirling Castle, fled to Europe, got pardoned in 1717 and returned to Glasgow. Clementina was mostly educated on the Continent, and became Roman Catholic. Clementina and Charles got to know each other. When Charles later heard, in 1752, that Clementina was at Dunkirk without any funds he sent Sir Henry Goring with fifty gold Louis and an offer: he was to procure her to come and live with him as his mistress in Ghent. Goring described Clementina as a 'bad woman' and did not like being used as 'no better than a pimp', so he left Charles's service. Clementina, however, did go to live with Charles for the next eight years. They moved to Liège where their only child, Charlotte, was born on 29 October 1753 and baptised as a Catholic. After putting up with years of abuse, Clementina left Charles, taking Charlotte with her. The young girl spent most of her life in French convents, estranged from Charles, who refused to officially recognise her. Unable to marry, she also became a mistress (of Ferdinand de Rohan, Archbishop of Bordeaux) and had several illegitimate children. Father and daughter were finally reconciled in 1784, when he legitimised Charlotte and created her Duchess of Albany. She left her own children with Clementina and became what we would now call her father's carer, dying less than two years after the Prince. Arguments still rage as to whether Charlotte's descendants are the rightful Stuart Kings of Scotland.

MORE PESTILENCE

PESTILENCES WEREN'T CONFINED to the late-medieval times. Goodness, no. Between 1818 and 1852, Glasgow suffered at least five outbreaks of typhus and two of cholera, all down to cramped living conditions and poor sanitation.

The 1818 typhus epidemic could be seen coming. Unlike typhoid, which is a *Salmonella* infection, typhus is caused by a form of *Rickettsia* carried around in human body lice – no point blaming rats this time. It had already been named 'the Irish disease' (a bit harsh, since they were not the cause but the most likely to be afflicted) when it hit London in 1817 and killed one in fourteen people. Typhus struck again – along with cholera – in 1826, and the town council had to buy extra ground to bury the victims. There was a further epidemic in 1843. None of this was helped by the huge influx of Highlanders after the clearances and Irish after the Great Famine of 1845. The pressure on the already-overcrowded housing and sanitation grew even worse.

Cholera, too, was apt to rampage through the city. The 1832 outbreak was a direct result of Glasgow's extensive trade with the East and killed 3,000 people (and across class boundaries too – unlike typhus, which at least had the good manners to afflict the lower orders). Glasgow's doctors were clear, by 1842, that there was a link between disease and sanitation, but it took further cholera epidemics in 1848 and 1853 to get much done about it.

After the 1843 epidemic, when more than 32,000 fever cases were reported and at least 1,300 victims died, a young Glasgow doctor named Robert Perry decided to publish his *Facts and Observations on the Sanitory* [sic] *State of Glasgow* and mapped the incidence throughout the city to show the relationship between disease and poverty. He drew a distinction between typhus and typhoid fever and pinned the blame on poor living conditions, lack of nourishing food and decent clothing, and the appalling state of the water.

Water, meanwhile, was in short supply. The booming industries used it but polluted it, and even though Glasgow's far-reaching and pioneering Police Act of 1800 started to regulate what we now call environmental services (paving, gas lighting, fire fighting and the obvious law and order, plus street cleaning

Above *Dr Robert Perry used the new science of statistics and a colour-coded map to show the connection between sanitation, poverty and disease when he published his* Facts and Observations on the Sanitory [sic] State of Glasgow *in 1844. Perry had the book printed by the Gartnavel Press, attached to what was then called the Royal Asylum for Lunatics, and 'in exercising the mental and bodily faculties of the inmates of the Lunatic Asylum, the Printing of this Paper, the Colouring the Maps, &c, is wholly the work of the inmates'.*

Right *Queen Victoria, who opened the new water supply in 1859. (Library of Congress, LC-USZ62-75994)*

and sewerage). It also established the first modern police force, the first detective service and the first use of police dogs – a pair of Airedales.

But clearly Glasgow needed more, and better, water. James Burn Russell, one of Glasgow's first medical health officers, used the new statutory registration of death, and cause of death, from 1855 to

Loch Katrine, source of Glasgow's water. (Library of Congress, LC-DIG-ppmsc-07686)

prove that clean water was needed. He also started vaccination schemes, and middens were taken away.

In October 1859 Queen Victoria opened the new water supply, which piped in supplies from Loch Katrine to Milngavie, the reservoir, and from there to Glasgow. Almost fifty miles of new sewer systems were laid between 1850 and 1875. Under the City Improvement Acts of the 1860s, many of the slums were bought with public money; they were cleared and replaced with better housing stock.

Then, in 1865, a few years after the water scheme, a surgeon at Glasgow Infirmary called Joseph Lister started washing his hands with carbolic acid before surgery and not operating in the same coat he wore for gardening. Antiseptics had arrived.

Clean water and better health were the consequences of all this, but the various outbreaks, disasters and associated financial problems all contributed to another set of conflicts – the Radical Riots and the Chartists.

It's a Riot!

GLASWEGIANS ARE REVOLTING – quite often, in fact! After the Great Fire of 1652, the town council set master crafts-men's wages at 1 merk per day, and 10 shillings for journeymen. Moreover, if the Glasgow masons, hammermen and other tradesmen were fully engaged then an employer could bring in workmen from elsewhere at the same rates. This was unpopular, to say the least – what's the point of having a burgess monopoly if you're going to let strangers come and work here, eh? On 5 February 1653 the wrights (carpenters) marched through the streets 'with cleukis and balstones in their hands', beat up any outsiders they found working and smashed up their workbenches and tools. This took four years to settle.

1725: LIQUOR TAX

When news reached Edinburgh, General Wade started to Glasgow and took over the city with a force of infantry, cavalry and artillery. Nineteen citizens were taken, bound and sent to Edinburgh for trial. Many Glasgow worthies were arrested, though they were quickly released. Damages were awarded to Mr Campbell, to the tune of £9,000. He chose to sell up and buy the island of Islay instead, although his descendants no longer own it.

It's worth noting, in passing, that at this time the Tolbooth was not just a gaol and the centre of Glasgow's administration but also a public house, and that the gaoler would lean over the half-door, looking for customers who wished to slake their drouth. Ah, the good old days!

1760: KEEP THE SABBATH!

Until this year, the old Presbyterian rule prevailed: no one could take a constitu-tional walk on the Sabbath, no lamps were lighted on Sunday evenings and all amuse-ments were banned.

Official 'compurgators' – clearly the model for Orwell's Thought Police – walked about the streets during holy service on Sundays and ordered offenders to stop enjoying themselves and go home, arresting them if they refused.

3 SEPTEMBER 1787: THE CALTON WEAVERS' STRIKE

When, in 1787, Nathaniel Jones produced the first *Directory of Glasgow*, little did he think that his fellow Glaswegians would be sorely libelled in the introduction to an 1887 reprint, written by someone who wisely chose to hide behind the pseudonym 'The Rambling Reporter'. This know-nowt described the 'common people' as:

> ...living in a state of ignorance, poverty, and semi-barbarism. In troublous times men went about the streets constantly armed; and it was not by any means uncommon for clergymen to appear in the pulpit fully equipped with deadly weapons, in the shape of swords, daggers, and pistols. Intestine feuds were every-day occurrences; and wrongs were righted on the 'good old rule,' by blood-letting and knocking each other on the head, in defiance of law or justice, except the law of self-preservation and the wild justice of revenge...

Dam' cheek! Anyway, 1787 certainly was a 'troublous time'. Glasgow's population had grown to about 60,000, and handloom weaving at home was the main occupation, after the collapse of the tobacco trade in 1776. The imminent French Revolution was driving home the message that People Power was possible.

Glasgow's muslin weavers were due to suffer a second pay cut in less than a year. After a number of local meetings, a larger rally was organised for 30 June at Glasgow

Soldiers opened fire on Glasgow's weavers as they headed towards the cathedral. (LC-DIG-ppmsc-07595)

Green. An estimated 7,000 weavers attended. The next week, the *Glasgow Mercury* carried a letter, purporting to be a unanimous resolution, sent by James Mirrie and the committee appointed by the weavers. It claimed that the price cut would amount to a reduction in wages of one quarter, and at a time when rents and other costs were rising – but that the protesters would not 'offer violence to any man or his work'. Then they went on strike.

This lasted the rest of June and through to October. It was concentrated in the weaving district of Calton, which was then just outside Glasgow's boundary. That meant that the city authorities had no power over them. But when, on Monday 3 September, a crowd of weavers gathered at the boundary of neighbouring Gallowgate, the lord provost arrived to disperse them. However, he and his force were driven back by bricks and stones. The weavers then meant to march to the cathedral, putting them within Glasgow's jurisdiction.

Colonel Kellet's 39th Regiment of Foot met the protesters near the Drygate. The troops opened fire, killing three weavers, mortally wounding three more and injuring many. Every soldier involved received a new pair of shoes and hose.

1799: RIOTS OVER BREAD PRICES

The city would not have to wait until 1811 for another riot, however. Times were changing for Glasgow. The city was now industrial and the days were past when everyone could keep a cow, a pig and some chickens in a kailyard. Now, they worked for wages and were at the mercy of shop and market prices. All it took was a war or a failed harvest to push the less well-heeled into poverty and near-starvation.

That was more or less what happened in 1799.

The last decade had been filled with incident:

- The French had executed their king, guillotined the aristocracy and set about destabilising Ireland, causing Britain to declare war.
- To make matters worse, a commercial crisis in 1793 had shattered three Glasgow banks and a number of companies, but Glasgow gaily went on over-paying ministers and white-washing church interiors, building roads, cleaning streets and the like.
- In 1793 an upstart artillery officer called Napoleon Bonaparte had driven the British out of Toulon and demolished the alliance with Spain, Prussia and Austria.
- In 1795, the city was called upon to send fifty-seven men for Navy service, or pay a levy: the total cost was over £1,000.
- In London, George III was subject to an assassination attempt to cries of 'bread' and 'peace'!
- In 1797 Glasgow offered to raise two battalions of infantry, 1,500 men in total. They were asked to raise about 640 men, but only managed to find nine, leading to another 'deficiency levy' of almost £1,400.
- There was a mutiny in the Royal Navy and the Bank of England nearly closed.
- The Irish, supported by the French General Humbert, were in uproar (but routed at Vinegar Hill in June 1798) and Glasgow contributed a further £1,000 for defence, plus £13,500 raised from among the inhabitants and 2,000 guineas subscribed by the 1st Battalion of the Royal Glasgow Volunteers. All of this was at a time when the Glasgow's

bill to the British Government for the Gallowgate barracks was unpaid to the tune of £2,000 and Glasgow's income from rents, dues, tolls and so on was less than £9,000.

Then the 1799 harvest failed.

Truly, humankind is three square meals and a box of matches away from total barbarism. The Glasgow militia had to stop the hungry from pillaging the granaries, and the town council had to pay dearly (almost £120,000) to import oats, wheat, barley, beans, pease, flour and potatoes. New Lanark philanthropist David Dale donated a shipload of corn from India (an unfamiliar item which the citizenry dubbed 'small peas'). Despite all this, a 'meal mob' riot broke out on 15 February 1800 and did a great deal of public and private injury. Fortunately, the 1801 harvest was the best anyone could remember, and the unrest stopped. But by then the 1800 Glasgow Police Act had established the first modern police force in Britain.

1809-1820:
THE WEAVERS ORGANISE!

The General Association of Operative Weavers was founded in 1809 and set about trying to improve wages and working conditions. The average weaver's wage had halved, which led to a general strike in 1813 when 40,000 weavers stayed out for more than two months.

In 1816 the 'Committee for Organising a Provisional Government', a secret body of Radicals, was formed to overthrow the government. Sadly it was awash with government spies, including Duncan Turner, a tin-smith, John Craig, a weaver, and Robert Lees, called only 'the Englishman'. The leading spy was

John King, an Anderston weaver, who attended a meeting at Marshall's Tavern in the Gallowgate on 21 March 1820 and managed to leave just before the rest of the committee was arrested. In their absence, King announced an armed uprising and posted a call for revolution all over the city on 1 April 1820. It asked the people of Glasgow to 'desist from their labour'.

Sad to say, it worked. Weavers and other workers all over west and central Scotland downed tools, refused to work and started arming and drilling themselves for conflict.

Three days later, Turner inveigled a group of about sixty men to march on the Carron Iron Works near Falkirk where they might arm themselves. Andrew Hardie was their leader, and he unwittingly led them into an ambush of soldiers from Perth. Four of the Radicals were wounded, and nineteen were taken as prisoners to Stirling Castle.

Other small uprisings were in hand all over the west and south of Scotland, but government always seemed to be ready for them. On 5 April the army occupied Glasgow, and James Wilson, leader of the Strathaven Radicals, was arrested, along with nine others. When the prisoners were being moved from Paisley on 8 April, however, the escorting soldiers were attacked by the citizens of Greenock. The soldiers retaliated by opening fire on the mob, killing or injuring eighteen people, including a child.

On 13 July 1820, Andrew Hardie was tried for High Treason at Stirling. Witnesses described to the court how he had seized a magistrate on the corner of Duke Street, declaring that he would 'lose the last drop of his blood before he would let him take [the proclamation] down'. Another man described seeing the rebellious weavers waving their hats at a party of cavalry at Bonnymuir before they 'ran down to a dyke (wall) at the foot of the hill, behind which they posted themselves in a stooping posture and began to fire on the troops in an irregular manner... [so that] he could see nothing afterwards but a cloud of smoke.'

The sentence, for Wilson, Hardie and Baird, was death. They were to be 'drawn on a hurdle to the place of execution, and be there hanged by the neck until they be dead; and that afterwards their heads be severed from their bodies, and their bodies (divided into four quarters) be disposed of as our Lord the King shall think fit.' Nineteen others, mainly weavers, were transported to the colonies – chiefly New South Wales, as America had declined to take any convicts since 1776. Hardie's grandson, Keir Hardie, became one of the founders of the Labour Party, so you could say it was in his blood – or at least, the family memory.

The next riot in Glasgow was not in the cause of worker's rights, but those of the dead.

1 MARCH 1823:
THE ANATOMY RIOTS

Until the Anatomy Act of 1832, surgeons who wanted cadavers for demonstrations and lectures to students could only get the bodies of executed murderers. These were relatively rare, and in high demand, so there was a degree of grave-robbing and even some do-it-yourself corpse-making, as the infamous activities of Burke and Hare in Edinburgh (pictured below) showed some four years later. This whole enterprise

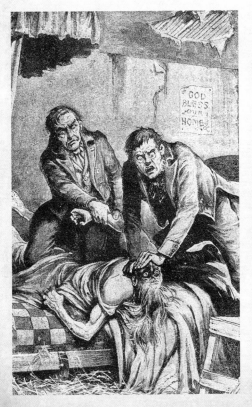

Correct Account of THE RIOTS
Concerning Stealing Dead Bodies, in
different parts of Glasgow on Saturday
and Sunday, the 1st and 2nd March,
1823; with an account of the Dead
Bodies, and the Heads, Limbs & Pieces of
Human Bodies Found.

Early on Friday night, the neighbourhood of the College Churchyard,
was alarmed by noises proceeding from
the churchyard, when the watchman
on that station sprung his rattle, and
having procured assistance, they entered
the graveyard, where they found three
doctors and a boy, whom they escorted to
the Police Office.

In the middle of the above night, the
watchman at Ladywell street remarked
two well-dressed persons hastening
toward the High Church-yard. An
interval of some minutes elapsed,
when he perceived the same persons
return, followed by some others bearing
something tied up in a large bundle.
An alarm was instantly given, when
the watchmen assembled, and having
secured the man who was bearing the
bundle, and a young man who appeared
of the same party, they then proceeded
to examine the bundle; which was
found to be the body of a man deceased,
who had lived in the Havannah, and
who was lately interred in the aforesaid
church yard. The fellow that carried
the corpse made such oppositions to his
being taken, by striking, kicking, and
biting the watchmen, that they thought
proper to bind him and the corpse
together, on a hurley, when they were
removed to the Office.

It was with great difficulty the police
could prevent the crowd that assembled
from taking vengeance on him. The son
of the man disinterred, appeared at the

horrified the general public, leading to the
erection of mort-safes – locked cages in
graveyards where the lately departed could
be left to putrefy for a few weeks until their
corpses were of no use to the anatomists.

At this point there were two medical
schools in Glasgow: the 'college' (Glasgow
University) and Anderson's University
(now Strathclyde). But it was the first of
these, then in High Street, that caused all
the bother. Just like the tabloids of today,
broadside printers vied to get horrific,
scandalous and sensational news to the
public – for a penny or two, of course – and
one from printers Mayne & Co. provides the
details of the arrest of bodysnatchers in
the 'college Churchyard', and the riot that
followed it.

Office some time afterwards, to claim his father's body.

Drawing conclusions from those and other events, it was that a great concourse of people assembled opposite a lecture room in Duke Street, on Saturday morning, at half past nine o'clock, when they proceeded to break open the door, when a most appalling scene presented itself. On the floor stood a large tub, in which was found a number of heads, arms and legs. On the table lay the whole body of a woman with long hair. The body of a man lay aside it with the head cut off, and the entrails out, and otherwise dissected. At the end of the room was a complete skeleton. Other mangled bodies were found, and limbs and mutilated fragments of bodies were strewed about the room. The mobs were so exasperated that, seizing the bodies and every thing found in the room, they tossed them into the streets. They were proceeding to demolish the premises until the arrival of Baillie Snell, with the Police, and a detachment of soldiers, when a proper guard was stationed to prevent farther violence.

Yesterday forenoon a crowd assembled in Portland Street at another lecture room, when they had proceeded to break the other door, and were proceeding to the room, when they were alarmed by the arrival of the Police. Some bones were found on the premises, and were tossed about by the crowd. Guards are placed to prevent mischief while a legal investigation is going on, to satisfy the public mind.

'The Havannah' refers to an area developed by Gavin Williamson in 1763. It was roughly where High Street Station is now, and was developed using the prize money that Williamson had been granted

for capturing the capital of Cuba, a feat he had completed during his time with the Navy. Just for the record, in 1863 Glasgow's Medical Officer of Health said in his report that: 'Havannah Street is not surpassed by any close in the city for filth, misery, crime and disease; it contains fifty-nine houses, all inhabited by a most wretched class of individuals; several of these houses do not exceed 15ft square, yet they are forced to contain a family of sometimes six persons.'

When the Resurrection Men were about their grisly trade, wealthier Glaswegians started to make use of mort-safes to protect their remains. Coffins were placed in these rented locked cages, which often had watchmen, for a few weeks until the body was past its best from the point of view of dissection. Then they would be properly interred. But some remained locked in for ever. This example is of paper manufacturer James Russell in the Ramshorn Graveyard in Ingram Street, who died in 1798.

1837:
THE COTTON-
SPINNERS' STRIKE

The 1830s was a time of depression every bit as bad as the more famous example a century later. Those who controlled weaving were again trying to cut wages, and Glasgow's cotton spinners went on strike throughout July and August 1837. A 'knob' (blackleg) worker was shot and the High Sheriff of Lanarkshire (the county containing the part of Glasgow north and east of the Clyde) panicked. It arrested five members of the Cotton Spinners' Union for treason.

They were due to be tried on 10 of November in Edinburgh, but some official chicanery got the prisoners moved, without anyone knowing, from Glasgow's Bridewell Gaol to Edinburgh and their trial postponed for seventeen days. Suffice it to say that they were convicted of crimes such as 'molestation' and 'conspiracy to keep wages up'. The charges were either upheld by the narrowest of margins or thrown out. Nevertheless, the prisoners were sentenced to be transported for seven years. They actually spent three years in the appalling conditions of the prison hulks at Woolwich, before being pardoned and released.

But the Cotton Spinners' Union folded from lack of funds after the expensive trial – which was probably the whole point of the exercise.

One of the upshots, if that's word, of the 1837 strike was the murder of John Smith, who was a 'nob' – he had continued to work at the lower wages offered by Henry Houldsworth and Sons, in defiance of the 'unlawful' association', as the trial papers call the Glasgow Operative Body of Cotton-Spinners, who had organised the walk-out.

While Smith and his wife were buying food on a Saturday night, he was shot in the back. Thomas Hunter, Peter Hacket, Richard M'Neil, James Gibb and William M'Lean 'or one or more of them… this they did with the wicked and felonious intent thereby of deterring other workmen from continuing in, or taking employment at such rate of wages'. Smith managed to make a deposition before dying, and a reward of £500 was offered for information leading to a conviction, plus a pardon for 'any accomplice, not being the person who actually fired the pistol, who shall give such information and evidence'. The five accused were transported for seven years.

The government was worried – there had been a 'great meeting on Glasgow Green' that required '100 horse and 100 foot patrol, independent of the police'. Nobs were assaulted, spinning-mills were set ablaze, a bomb was thrown into a manufacturer's house and another spinner had vitriol (sulphuric acid) thrown in his face. James Corkindale MD, a surgeon at the Royal Infirmary, described an acid attack during an earlier strike in 1825 on spinner Neil M'Callum in these terms: 'I found the upper parts of his cheeks in an excoriated state, as if scalded; the eyelids were much swollen and discharging purulent matter; the eyes themselves were a good deal inflamed, and the part naturally transparent rendered opaque.'

He described another such attack on Charles Cairney: 'the half of his face and the half of his scalp became an ulcerated surface; thick patches of mortified parts falling off in succession…'

AD 1841

ALLAN PINKERTON AND THE CHARTISTS

CHARTISM WAS A working-class movement which demanded universal male suffrage, a secret ballot, no property qualification for members of Parliament, pay for members of Parliament, and annual elections for Parliament.

The origins of the 1841 Chartist demonstration was an address by Feargus O'Connor, a rabble-rouser recently released from York Gaol and the only ever Chartist MP. But there was an earlier episode, in 1838, connected with Allan Pinkerton, founder of the Chicago-based detective agency which bore his name. This gives us a chance to correct the common errors in most of the biographies.

Pinkerton was born on either 21 July or 21 August 1819 (the parish record is unclear, but the date was certainly not 25 August, as is usually claimed). His birthplace was in the Gorbals, on the corner of Rutherglen Loan and Muirhed Street. This area did not survive into the twentieth century and is now overtaken by Old Rutherglen Road, but it is not the site of Glasgow Central Mosque, as is often said – that was raised on the land occupied by Thomson's Mill, where Allan's mother and

Birthplace of Pinkerton. (Library of Congress, LC-DIG-PPMSCA-10784)

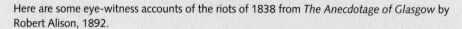

Here are some eye-witness accounts of the riots of 1838 from *The Anecdotage of Glasgow* by Robert Alison, 1892.

'In the year 1848,' states Mr. Daniel Frazer, 'I witnessed from the doorway of No. 113 (Buchanan Street), a procession of a large body of ill-fed, ill-clad, and half-armed Chartists, men, women, and boys, enter Buchanan Street by Royal Bank Place. After marching from the Green and Gallowgate, by East George Street and Queen Street, without much interruption, the procession turned sharp down the street, and when passing Gordon Street fired two shots in the air. At this moment I saw a Glasgow gentleman, a medical man, if my memory serves me right, rush into the procession and disarm one or two of the men who had fired the shots, and who were thus trying to overawe our civic authorities.

'Happily for law and order, nothing tended more to restore both than the speedy enrolment of a large force of special constables, composed greatly of our merchant princes. These gentlemen were all provided with substantial batons, and were for a time subjected to daily drill. They were stationed in the Royal Exchange, and elsewhere during the night.

'"An old Glasgow merchant and Sabbath school teacher, who himself acted as a special constable [communicated]... the following particulars:–

"This outbreak soon assumed an alarming aspect. The mob had rapidly increased while passing towards the west of the city; the streets got blocked, and shops were entered and robbed by the hungry people. Among others the premises of a gunsmith in Exchange Square were entered, and guns and ammunition carried off. The shots fired in Buchanan Street greatly alarmed the inhabitants, who hurriedly shut the doors of their shops. Many windows were broken, and their contents carried off. A set of silver-plated dish covers, and an epergne were taken from the window of Findlay & Field, jewellers, 72 Buchanan Street. A porter's hand-barrow – stolen from a grocer's door in George Street – was drawn in the procession by a young woman well-known to the police for her lawless habits as Biddy. On it was a sack of meal, a box of tea, some loaves of bread, etc. The silver plate was at once put on the top of this heap and carried off in triumph by Biddy, till she and her booty were lost sight of in Argyle Street.

'"...I was," continues Mr. Frazer's informant, "one of the special constables who escorted the wounded up the High Street to the Royal Infirmary. I was also afterwards applied to, as the Sabbath school teacher in St. Enoch's Wynd district, to assist the police in finding out Biddy's plunder. Knowing her to be of weak mind, and that she must have been used as a tool by others, I only consented to aid the police in the matter on getting their assurance that she should not be punished.

'"Armed with this assurance I entered Biddy's home, in a building well known as the Ark in St. Enoch's Wynd, and which had once been used as a maltbarn. Here, in a miserable attic room, I found Biddy's mother. She at first stoutly denied her daughter's complicity in the robbery, but on getting my assurance that no punishment would follow the acknowledgment of the crime, I was asked to look out a skylight window, and, on doing so, I saw the tea, the silver plate, etc., spread out on the roof. These were duly returned to their owners, and Biddy was allowed to go free."'

Armed police and demonstrators fighting in the Garscube Road during the 1880 Irish home rule riots, as depicted in the Illustrated London News. *Perhaps Mr McGee's fine emporium selling Irish Whiskey contributed to the high feelings.*

half-sisters worked. More appropriately, his house is now the offices of the procurator fiscal (chief prosecutor) for Glasgow and Strathkelvin. One day someone will find it appropriate to nail a plaque to its wall or erect a statue pointing this out.

By 1837, young Allan had his journeyman cooper's ticket, the same year Princess Victoria got her Queen's ticket and took over the family business of ruling the Empire. They both picked a bad year. The 1832 Reform Act and an economic downturn persuaded the mill owners to cut wages by half and the workers to down tools in protest. This sparked mass meetings and the formation of the National Radical Association. A year later, John Collins of the Birmingham Chartists arrived in Glasgow like a missionary, and plans were made for

an event on Monday 21 May on Glasgow Green. This was no storming-the-Bastille exercise: a procession of over seventy unions, with forty-odd of their marching bands, arrived ready for a day of speechifying to be followed by a 'soireé'. It was a gala, and anywhere between 30,000 (Tory estimate) and 200,000 (Radical estimate) turned up for a rather orderly meeting.

The young Pinkerton took part in the organisation of various social reform schemes to do with poverty, housing, sanitation and – interestingly, in the light of his later career – slavery. But whether he actually attended the occasion at Glasgow Green is in doubt, because he spent a lot of 1838 tramping the roads of southern Scotland and northern England to find cooper's work.

Allan Pinkerton (left) with President Abraham Lincoln.

Come the end of 1838, the general enthusiasm for Radicalism had waned somewhat, but Allan Pinkerton joined the Glasgow Universal Suffrage Association and became a director. Like most idealistic mass movements in Scotland, as soon as a body is established it flies apart like shrapnel. The Reformed Church ended up in splinters, its various secessions themselves fragmenting even more; Jacobitism became Catholics on one hand and Episcopalians on the other, and likewise Radicalism soon found itself in factions concerned variously with Temperance, Irish Home Rule, the various flavours of emerging Socialism, violence versus non-violence, and sundry other anarchies. The idealistic Pinkerton met, and was influenced by, George Julian Harney, an associate of Marx and Engels and later founder of the *Democrat* and *Red Republican* newspapers. This led him to participate in the unholy mess that was the Newport Rising on 4 November 1839. Had he and the other Glasgow men there been arrested, Pinkerton would have found himself transported to Australia. Instead, he got back to a Glasgow to find his association in the hands of a middle-class tea merchant and a rather well-off steam-engine mechanic.

Virtually accused of financial impropriety with the association's finances (and held liable for its debts, as a director), Pinkerton engaged in an exchange of frankly libellous letters to newspapers, and then resigned to set up his own Northern Democratic Association. He espoused physical force as the road to Reform, and watched with some satisfaction as the Suffrage Association fell to pieces.

At a fundraiser in 1841, organised by Allan, a young soprano sang and captivated him. She was an apprentice bookbinder from Paisley called Joan Carfrae, and they started 'winching'. There was more foment on the way, though. A poor harvest and a harsh winter prompted a wave of emigration that had the newspapers fretting about what would now be called a brain drain, as the skilled and talented headed for Canada and the United States, to be replaced by Irish who couldn't afford an Atlantic crossing and headed for the west of Scotland instead.

The Pinkerton myth talks of pursuit by the police, a tip-off by a sheriff's officer who had known his father and a hasty marriage followed by flight on a ship just ahead of the hue-and-cry. He may have been disillusioned by the failure to win universal suffrage (he was almost ninety years ahead of his time in that) and the internecine strife of Chartism and Radicalism. But the simple explanation may be that Allan sought a better life for his new wife in Quebec. At least one of his brothers was already in North America. He may have been escaping from the Glasgow slums, called at the time 'the filthiest in Britain'. While there were certainly arrests of militants in Glasgow, there is no evidence that Pinkerton was sought. The 'secret wedding' fantasised by many biographers was in fact celebrated publicly on 13 March 1842 in Glasgow Cathedral, after proclamation of banns on the previous three Sundays, and along with a number of other couples.

Joan Carfrae, it should be noted, was only fifteen at the time, and both she and Allan are given as residing in Glasgow (though neither was), which might suggest they were lying low, but possibly only from Mr and Mrs Carfrae. It then took them almost another month to 'flee' aboard a ship, on 8 April.

Many adventures followed: a storm, a shipwreck off Nova Scotia and the loss to predatory natives of all their possessions – including a brand-new wedding ring. The pair decided to forget Canada in favour of a bustling, brawling frontier town just developing on the shores of Lake Michigan. It was called Chicago, and it was fast becoming the place where everything was packaged up for the drive west to open up new country. What Chicago used was barrels – so what Chicago needed, clearly, was a barrel maker.

Other myths surrounding Pinkerton are that his father, William, is variously said to have died in 1826, 1828 or 1833, killed in a Chartist riot, and was the first sergeant in the Glasgow police. None of that is correct. Glasgow did indeed have a police force from 1800 (the first in Britain, despite what the London Metropolitan. will say) but William Pinkerton does not seem to have been part of it, nor was he the first sergeant – that singular honour belongs to a Donald MacLean. William does seem to have secured a position as a trusty (locker-up) at Glasgow City Gaol, and he was certainly built for the robust policing of the day, being unusually tall for the time at over 6ft and grim of countenance. Possibly, William had supplemented his weaving income as one of the 'Charlies' (nightwatchmen-cum-streetsweepers) which evolved in 1808 into a regular police force in the Gorbals, which was then a separate burgh. The Gorbals' men, however, would be drafted in to help Glasgow at times of need, such as Hogmanay, the Glasgow Fair holiday and major gatherings. References in some biographies to William's tenure as a police sergeant and an earlier career in the Black Watch (the 42nd Highland Regiment) are a confusion with Allan's elder half-brother, also William (born 1803), who did both of those things. The ex-army 'Big Hieland Polis' is something of a fixture in Glasgow's history, right up to the 1960s. It was said of them that they preferred to arrest people in Hope Street or Bath Street, as both were easier to spell than 'Sauchiehall'.

There is also confusion over Allan's father's injury and death. The 1841 census shows William alive and breathing in 1841 although Oliver Wendell Holmes, no less, has him paralysed during a Chartist riot in 1829 and dead in 1833, the dates now enshrined in the *Dictionary of American Biography*; Sigmond Lavine, writing in 1963, kills him off in 1829; James Horan, in 1967, has William die in a riot of 1827; and Dr James Mackay seems to accept a date between 1831 and 1833, based on the evidence of missing records from that date. But of large-scale riots in Glasgow in the late 1820s there is not a single record, and the mass gatherings of 1838 and 1841 were rather good-humoured affairs. In any case, the very term 'Chartist' only originated in 1838 with the publication of the People's Charter and was a reaction to the half-hearted electoral reforms of 1832 rather than a wages movement.

The whole story may be another invention of the fertile fictive brain of Allan Pinkerton, who published, late in his life, a series of dressed-up 'true-crime' yarns.

However, 1848 was the year that 100,000 people gathered on Glasgow Green to support the Reformist group generally called Chartists; Glasgow Cross was barricaded and many shops were plundered by the unemployed.

LISTER AND SURGERY IN GLASGOW

LOTS OF PLACES lay claim to Joseph Lister (1827-1912). He was born in Upton, Essex. He was Professor of Clinical Surgery at Edinburgh in 1869, and Professor of Surgery at King's College, London, in 1877.

However, he was Professor of Surgery at Glasgow from 1860, and visiting surgeon at Glasgow Royal Infirmary in 1861 – and it was at Glasgow, in 1865, that he started experimenting with carbolic acid to prevent infections in compound fractures, which led to the revolutionary concept of antiseptic surgery.

Surgery at that time was a brutal affair, and as many people died from the attentions of its practitioners as were saved by them – the actual death of Edward Drummond, described later in this book, is thought to be more likely due to misman-agement by the surgical profession than from the bullet which struck him.

Lister knew that many people survived a wound or an operation but died later of what was called 'ward fever'. There had already been a suggestion that cleanliness and post-operative recovery were linked: Ignaz Semmelweiss, a doctor in Budapest, started insisting that his colleagues should wash their hands with calcium chloride after operations and between patients, and possibly not carry out operations in the same filthy coats they used for gardening or dissection. Up to this time, a dirty coat was a sort of sign of a surgeon's experience, and the smell was called the 'good old surgical stink'.

Although deaths on Semmelweiss's wards plummeted after this innovation, he had annoyed the conservative elite of Hungarian medicine by asking them to accept something new, so his work was ignored. Semmelweiss died in 1865, ironi-cally of blood poisoning – but later they did name the Budapest medical university after him, so never mind, eh?

That very year (1865), Joseph Lister read about the work of Louis Pasteur on the anaerobic souring of wine and the role of 'microbes' in the air – could they not also carry diseases in hospital wards? Lister decided to clean his patient's wounds thor-oughly, then cover them with lint doused in a solution of carbolic acid (phenol). He first used this on compound fractures, where the broken bone penetrates the skin (leaving a bare wound open to 'microbes' so that gangrene could set in). He also insisted

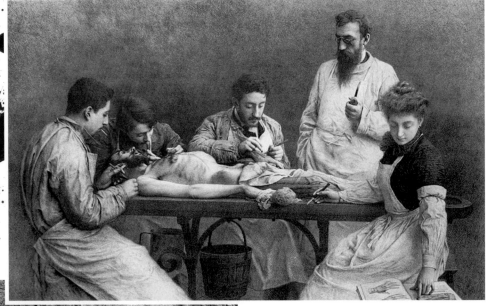

Above *A dissection – notice the filth, lack of gloves and smoking!*
Below *Statue of Lister in Kelvingrove Park.*

on the revolutionary practice of cleaning the operating instruments. Survival rates rocketed.

Lister had the even better idea of air-to-air combat – he used a pump to spray a fine mist of phenol into the air of the operating theatre and around the patient. Again, it was a remarkable success, and the number of his surgical patients who died plummeted.

Lister became a baronet in 1883 and was raised to the peerage in 1883 as 1st Baron Lister. He died in 1912 at Walmer in Kent, hailed as the 'Father of Antiseptic Surgery'.

And, by the way, Lister's friend, Dr Sam Gamgee, took his ideas further by developing an aseptic dressing called Gamgee tissue, but is better remembered as giving his name to a hobbit – cotton wool was still known in the Birmingham of Tolkien's youth as 'Gamgee'.

LISTER'S GLASGOW CASES

In the *Lancet* of 1867, Lister wrote up his cases under the title 'On a new method of treating compound fracture, abscess, etc. With observations on the conditions of suppuration.' Two typical cases are described below:

Case 1: 'James G., aged eleven years, was admitted into the Glasgow Royal Infirmary on the 12th of August, 1865, with compound fracture of the left leg, caused by the wheel of an empty cart passing over the limb a little below its middle. The wound, which was about an inch and a half long, and three quarters of an inch broad, was close to, but not exactly over, the line of fracture of the tibia.'

Case 2: 'Patrick F., a healthy labourer, aged thirty-two, had his right tibia broken on the afternoon of the 11th of September, 1865, by a horse kicking him with its full force over the anterior edge of the bone about its middle. He was at once taken to the infirmary, where Mr Miller, the house surgeon in charge, found a wound measuring about an inch by a quarter of an inch, from which blood was welling profusely. He put up the fracture in pasteboard splints, leaving the wound exposed between their anterior edges, and dressing it with a piece of lint dipped in carbolic acid, large enough to overlap the sound skin about a quarter of an inch in every direction. In the evening he changed the lint for another piece, also dipped in carbolic acid, and covered this with oiled paper. I saw the patient next day, and advised the daily application of a bit of lint soaked in carbolic acid over the oiled paper; and this was done for the next five days. On the second day there was an oozing of red fluid from beneath the dressing, but by the third day this had ceased entirely. On the fourth day, when, under ordinary circumstances, suppuration would have made its appearance, the skin had a nearly natural aspect, and there was no increase of swelling, while the uneasiness he had previously felt was almost entirely absent. His pulse was 64, and his appetite improving. On the seventh day, though his general condition was all that could be wished, he complained again of some uneasiness, and the skin about the still adherent crust of blood, carbolic acid, and lint was found to be vesicated, apparently in consequence of the irritation of the carbolic acid.

From the seventh day the crust was left untouched till the eleventh day, when I removed it, disclosing a concave surface destitute of granulations, and free from suppuration. Water

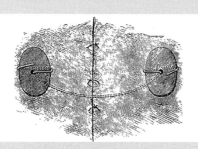

Lister pioneered a method of sewing people back together using lead buttons and silver wire as thread.

dressing was now applied, and by the sixteenth day the entire sore, with the exception of one small spot where the bone was bare, presented a healthy granulating aspect, the formation of pus being limited to the surface of the granulations.

I now had occasion to leave Glasgow for some weeks, and did so feeling that the cure was assured. On my return, however, I was deeply mortified to learn that hospital gangrene attacked the sore soon after I went away, and made such havoc that amputation became necessary.'

MURDER, POLIS!

1843: DANIEL M'NAGHTEN – DELUSIONALLY INSANE, OR HIRED ASSASSIN?

Rarely does someone get into the law books because something crucial is named after him or her. The M'Naghten Rules, which govern the legal test of criminal insanity, are an exception.

Daniel M'Naghten or McNaughton (1813-1865) was, he claimed, born in Glasgow, the illegitimate son of a local woodturner and public-house landlord, also called Daniel M'Naghten. When his mother died he went to be an apprentice to his father at his workshop in Stockwell Street, but after working as a journeyman he was not offered a place in the business. The young M'Naghten left, tried acting for three years, and then went back to Glasgow in 1835 to set up his own (fairly successful) woodwork shop, first in Turners Court and then back in Stockwell Street. He was, by all accounts, sober, hard-working and thrifty, and attended the Glasgow Mechanic's Institute and the Athenaeum (a debating society-cum-education institution), learned French and took to Radical politics, associating himself with the Chartists.

M'Naghten sold his business in late 1840. He spent two years in London, France and Glasgow (where he attended anatomy lectures) but then started telling people, including his father, the Glasgow police, and his Member of Parliament, that he was being spied on and followed around by Tories. Everyone thought he was, as they say in Glasgow, 'wannert' (meaning wandered or delusional).

For some reason, M'Naghten was in London on 20 January 1843, having just deposited £750 in a bank. He had been seen acting suspiciously around Whitehall, and on that day he walked up behind Edward Drummond, private secretary to Prime Minister Robert Peel, and shot him. A police constable overpowered him. It transpired that M'Naghten thought he had shot Peel himself. Drummond walked away and had the bullet extracted, but died five days later of complications.

At his first appearance at Bow Street Magistrates' Court the morning after the shooting, M'Naghten described his 'persecution' by agents and spies of the Tories (though he never referred to this again). Police Inspector J.M. Tierney gave evidence from his notes:

Daniel M'Naghten, looking every bit the staring-eyed madman.

The prisoner after being cautioned as to his statement, says, 'The Tories in my native city have driven me to this, and have followed me to France, Scotland, and other parts; I can get no sleep from the system they pursue towards me; I believe I am driven into a consumption by them; they wish to murder me. That is all I wish to say at present; they have completely disordered me, and I am quite a different man than before they commenced this annoyance towards me.'

The defence – paid for by his father, out of the mysterious £750 from the bank – presented witnesses to M'Naghten's strange behaviour before the crime. The prosecution offered no evidence regarding his state of mind, and Chief Justice Tindal told the jury that if they found the prisoner not guilty on grounds of insanity, he would be taken proper care of. Not even bothering to retire, the jury duly returned that verdict. It was controversial and even Queen Victoria – no stranger to assassination attempts – told her prime minister in no uncertain terms what she thought. The rules were tightened up so that 'insanity' required that the accused should not 'know the nature and quality of the act he was doing or, if he did know it that he did not know that what he was doing was wrong'.

M'Naghten was sent to the State Criminal Lunatic Asylum at Bethlem Hospital (known colloquially as 'Bedlam') for twenty-one years, where he was classified as an 'imbecile' and developed diabetes and heart problems. In 1864 he was sent to the brand-new Broadmoor Asylum, where, on admission, he was described as 'a native of Glasgow, an intelligent man'. He died the next year.

But where did the £750 come from? It would be worth 100 times that today. Was M'Naghten actually a politically-motivated terrorist financed to assassinate the prime minister and capable of feigning insanity when it went wrong? In which case, was he really being followed around by 'spies of the Tories', who had an inkling of his intentions?

The jury is still out on that one.

1857: DID MADELEINE SMITH POISON PIERRE L'ANGELIER?

This case had everything: sex, high society, scandal, a dastardly Frenchman, a jilted fiancé, and a phial of poison – and if she did it, well, then she got away with it. You couldn't make it up.

Pierre Emile L'Angelier wasn't actually French, but from the Channel Islands.

The Residence of Madeleine Smith, Blythswood Square, Glasgow.
(Now the offices of the British Legal Life Assurance Co.)
The window of Miss Smith's bedroom is the second area window in the side street. The door to Mr. Minnoch's house is the one a little further down in the same block.

He was, however, a Mellors-type figure, working as an apprentice nurseryman. Madeleine Hamilton Smith (1835-1928) was the eldest daughter of a wealthy architect (as was her mother) with a grand town house in Blythswood Square, Glasgow, and a country estate near Rhu, Helensburgh.

Against all conventions of the day, Madeleine began a secret affair with L'Angelier early in 1855. They exchanged many letters, met at her bedroom window and in the woods near the family's country house and eventually consummated their passion. She promised to marry the handsome gardener. Unaware of all this (of course), Madeleine's parents arranged for her to meet a suitable match – one William Harper Minnoch, a solidly upper-middle-class chap. In February 1857, Madeleine tried to break off the liaison with L'Angelier and asked for her letters back. Spotting the main chance, L'Angelier threatened to release the letters and expose her unless she married him as promised. She was then

seen at a pharmacy buying arsenic and signing the poison book 'M.H. Smith'. On 23 March 1857, L'Angelier died from arsenic poisoning. Madeleine's letters to him were discovered in his boarding house in Franklin Place, and Madeleine was arrested for murder. Open and shut case, your honour!

Or possibly not. Madeleine was ably defended by advocate John Inglis, Lord Glencorse, who would, eight years later, preside over the Pritchard case. The evidence was circumstantial but damning. She had bought arsenic in the weeks leading up to Emile's death, and she had both motive and opportunity. But the jury found that the prosecution had not made a firm enough case and returned that peculiarly Scottish verdict 'not proven' – which basically means 'we know you did it, but they haven't proved it'. Furthermore, there was felt to be some jiggery-pokery about letters and envelopes which were undated but which the police had probably arranged so as to best suit their case. Also, no eyewitness could be found to testify that Madeleine and L'Angelier had met in the weeks leading up to his death. And why shouldn't a young woman buy arsenic? It was used as a cosmetic, after all.

However, the scandal was such that Madeleine Smith left Scotland, initially for England. On 4 July 1861 she married George Wardle, an artist and business manager to William Morris. They had a son and a daughter but later separated, and Madeleine moved to New York City. She took the name Lena Wardle Sheehy, and died there in 1928, a highly respected member of New York society.

Pierre lies in the Ramshorn graveyard, Glasgow.

But don't take my word for it – watch David Lean's 1950 film *Madeleine*.

1865: PRITCHARD THE POISONER

There is no doubt that Dr Edward Pritchard deserved to dangle on a rope for the killing of his wife, mother-in-law and possibly one other woman, but some of the more colourful allegations that later sprang up around him are no more than that.

Pritchard was a strange-looking chap – he had a corker of a beard, for a start – with some unconventional habits. Born in 1825, he claimed to have a number of doubtful medical qualifications, possibly from King's College, London, or perhaps from Leyden University. He became an assistant surgeon in the Royal Navy in 1846 and managed to serve on the *Victory* in its last days. Four years later, Pritchard left the Navy and married Mary Jane Taylor, daughter of a retired and rather well-off Edinburgh silk merchant. In 1851 he took up a position as GP and medical officer in Hunmanby, Yorkshire, but left under a cloud of some sort – possibly involving debt, and his propensity for riding up to church on a Sunday and horsewhipping his patients. He moved to Glasgow, taking up residence in Berkeley Terrace in 1860 with wife, mother-in-law and five children.

A boaster and a liar, Pritchard also considered himself the great lover. This may account for his first murder. On 5 May 1863, Pritchard's house caught fire and the family's twenty-five-year-old servant girl, Elizabeth McGrain, was killed. The fire had started in her room but she had made no attempt to escape – so it is likely that Elizabeth was unconscious, sedated or perhaps already dead. The procurator fiscal thought as much – possibly suspecting Pritchard of starting the fire to cover up a rape and murder – but no charges were brought.

Two years later, and now living in Sauchiehall Street, Pritchard went one better by poisoning first his seventy-year-old mother-in-law, Jane Taylor, and then his wife barely a month later. A colleague, Dr Paterson, who was helping to treat Jane for a mysterious illness, was extremely suspicious and refused to sign the death certificates. Paterson may or may not have been the author of the anonymous letter sent to the authorities which resulted in the bodies being exhumed. They were found to be loaded with the poisonous mineral antimony.

Pritchard tried to pin the blame on a housemaid (he was probably having an affair with her, which may have been his motive for the killings), but he was convicted after a five-day hearing in Edinburgh in July 1865, presided over by John Inglis, Lord Glencorse – the same man who, as an advocate, had defended Madeleine Smith eight years earlier, so

Pritchard and his impressive beard.

presumably he knew a thing or two about poisoners. A statement was released shortly afterwards from Glasgow Gaol.

> Confession by Edward William Pritchard, and made in the presence of an All-seeing God, and the Rev. T. Watson Reid, my present spiritual adviser, on the 19th day of July, 1865, at Glasgow Prison, for communication to the proper authorities. I, Edward William Pritchard, in the full possession of all my senses, and understanding this awful position in which I am placed, do make free and open confession that the sentence commuted on me is just; that I am guilty of the death of my mother-in-law, Mrs Taylor, and of my wife, Mary Jane Pritchard; that I can assign no motive for the conduct which actuated me beyond a species of terrible madness and my use of ardent spirits. I hereby freely and fully state that the confession made to Rev. R.S. Oldman on the 11th day of this month was not true, and I hereby confess that I alone, not Mary McLeod, poisoned my wife in the way brought out in evidence at my trial.

At 8 a.m. on 28 July he gained the dubious honour of being the last person publicly executed in Glasgow when he was hanged in front of an estimated 80,000 not-well-wishers on Glasgow Green.

Even Michael Jackson, who played live at Glasgow Green, could only draw 35,000 in 1992 – but then that was a ticketed affair. It is said that the coffin Pritchard was taken away in was so ill-made that he fell out of the bottom – and some enterprising local liberated his boots.

After the hanging, the whole 'Pritchard the Poisoner' industry got into full swing, as it were. Books, magazine articles, 'revelations' and other materials sprang up. He even made it into Conan Doyle's *Adventure of the Speckled Band* (1892), in which Holmes says to Watson that when a doctor goes bad 'he is the first of criminals', and that Pritchard and another poisoner (William Palmer) were 'at the head of their profession'.

In 1947 the renowned Scottish playwright James Bridie penned *Dr Angelus*, based on the Pritchard case, definitely written for and originally starring Alastair Sim.

OTHER GLASGOW POISONERS?

We can discount Dr Thomas Neill Cream (1850-1892), the Lambeth Poisoner, who – although born in Glasgow – was raised in Quebec, to where his family emigrated when he was four, and did his best work in Chicago and England. But he may have had other victims in Canada and Scotland. Cream, who preferred strychnine as a method of dispatch, was executed after he tried to pin the blame for his crimes on others.

He also confessed to being Jack the Ripper, although he was in prison in America at the time the Whitechapel murders took place.

LAST WOMAN HANGED

Susan Newell was the last woman hanged in Scotland, at Duke Street prison on 10 October 1923. Newell, then aged thirty, strangled and killed a thirteen-year-old newspaper boy, John Johnston, because he called at her flat and would not give her the evening paper without her paying for it. After she killed him, Newell went to sleep. She then wheeled his body through the streets in a cart covered by a rug, with her young daughter, Janet, perched on top. It was her daughter's evidence which convicted her: Newell had told Janet to pin the blame on her stepfather, who inconveniently had an alibi, but she refused.

Weirdly, Newell accepted a lift from a kindly lorry-driver, who failed to notice the boy's leg sticking out from the rug. Fortunately, a woman passer-by did, and called the police.

The jury at her trial felt that she might be insane, convicted her on a majority verdict and unanimously recommended mercy.

She was the first woman to hang in Scotland since Jessie King in 1889, and although there was considerable public sympathy for a reprieve, the Secretary of State for Scotland felt that her crime was more serious than that of Edith Thompson, who had been hanged in England less than a year earlier for a not so serious crime, and so he couldn't be seen to wimp out on this one.

As an interesting aside, the usual hangman, John Ellis, did not like hanging women, and there was a problem of some kind each time he did (such as with Emily Swann and Edith Thompson in England). In this case, Ellis failed to pin her wrists fully, concentrating instead on a leather belt around the legs, apparently to prevent her skirts billowing up as she dropped. The proprieties must be observed, after all. On the gallows, Newell refused the customary white hood, saying to Ellis, 'Don't put that thing over me'. She has the fame of being perhaps the calmest person ever to be executed. She never admitted her guilt.

There are a couple of crimes for which people were hanged in Scotland which don't even appear in the English law books. One was 'stouthrief' (robbery in a house), and the other is 'hamesucken' ('the seeking and invasion of a person in his dwelling house', in other words, entering a house with the intent of doing harm to the occupant).

PETER MANUEL, SERIAL KILLER

By far the most notorious Glasgow murderer was Peter Manuel, who admitted to killing eighteen people. He was charged with, and convicted for, eight murders across Lanarkshire and the south of Scotland between 1956 and his arrest in January 1958. One case was dropped and another, in England, was attributed to him after his execution.

He was born Peter Thomas Anthony Manuel on 13 March 1927 in New York, USA, to Scottish parents who lived in Detroit. They returned to live in Birkenshaw, Lanarkshire, when Manuel was five years old. He was nicknamed 'the Beast of Birkenshaw' by the newspapers while still unidentified. Manuel was hanged in Barlinnie on 11 July 1958, the second-last man to die on those gallows, and the third-last in Scotland.

A known petty thief while still a child, Manuel committed a number of sexual attacks that got him nine years in Peterhead, along with several other

The prison photograph of Peter Manuel, courtesy of the National Records of Scotland.

GLASGOW HANGINGS

There have been twenty-two executions by hanging in Glasgow in the twentieth century: twelve at Duke Street prison before its closure in 1955, and then ten at Barlinnie, known locally as the Bar-L. These were:

Duke St

Date	Name	Age	Victim(s)	Hangman
12 Nov. 1902	Patrick Leggett	30	S.J. Leggett	W. Billington
26 July 1904	Thomas Gunning	48	Agnes Allen	W. Billington
14 Nov. 1905	Pasha Liffey	20	M. Jane Welsh	H. Pierrepoint
16 May 1917	Thos McGuiness	34	Alexander Imlach	John Ellis
11 Nov. 1919	James Adams	31	Mary Doyle (Kane)	John Ellis
26 May 1920	A. James Fraser	24	Henry Senior	John Ellis
26 May 1920	James Rollins	23	Henry Senior	John Ellis
21 Feb. 1922	William Harkness	31	Eliz. Benjamin	John Ellis
10 October 1923	Susan Newell	30	John Johnston	John Ellis
24 Sept. 1925	John Keen	22	Noorh Mohammed	T. Pierrepoint
24 January 1928	James McKay	40	Agnes Arbuckle	R. Baxter
03 August 1928	George Reynolds	40	Thomas Lee	R. Baxter

Barlinnie

Date	Name	Age	Victim(s)	Hangman
06 April 1946	Patrick Carraher	40	John Gordon	T. Pierrepoint
08 Feb.1946	John Lyon	21	John Brady	T. Pierrepoint
10 August 1946	John Caldwell	20	James Straiton	A. Pierrepoint
30 Oct. 1950	Chris. Harris	28	Martin Dunleavy	A. Pierrepoint
16 Dec.1950	James Robertson	31	Cath. McCluskey	A. Pierrepoint
12 April 1952	James Smith	21	Martin J. Malone	A. Pierrepoint
29 May 1952	Pat. G. Deveney	42	J. Deveney	A. Pierrepoint
26 Jan. 1953	Geo. Fran. Shaw	25	M. Connolly	A. Pierrepoint
11 July 1958	Peter Manuel	31	Marion Hunter, McDonald Watt, Vivienne Isabella, Reid Watt, Margaret Hunter Brown, Isabelle Wallace Cooke, Peter James Smart, Doris Smart, Michael Smart	H. Allan
22 December 1960	Anthony Miller	19	John Cremin	H. Allan

The last executions by hanging took place in 1964, before capital punishment was abolished for murder in Great Britain in 1969 (1973 in Northern Ireland). The death penalty remained for certain other offences (for example, treason, setting fire to a Naval dockyard, piracy and certain military crimes) until 1998 at the latest, although it was never used.

sentences. But in 1956 he started killing. His victims were:

Anne Kneilands (seventeen) on 2 January 1956, at East Kilbride golfcourse; his father provided an alibi but, although he confessed, the case was dropped for lack of evidence.

Marion Watt (forty-five), Vivienne Watt (sixteen) and Margaret Brown (forty-one) on 17 September 1956, a mother, daughter and sister shot to death at their home in Burnside, Glasgow, while Manuel was out on bail for a colliery burglary.

Marion's husband, William Watt, was arrested. He was released two months later, but remained the prime suspect until the Smart family were shot in 1958.

Sydney Dunn (thirty-six), shot and killed on 8 December 1957 while driving his taxi in Newcastle, where Manuel was looking for work. He wouldn't be tied to the murder until two weeks after he was hanged, when a button found in Dunn's taxi was matched to a jacket belonging to Manuel.

Isabelle Cooke (seventeen), who disappeared on 28 December 1957 after

---

Last Whipping through Glasgow by the Last Glasgow Hangman.

On the afternoon of Sunday, 17th February, 1822, a most extraordinary riot took place in the city.

It was directed against Mr. George Provand, oil and colour merchant, who then occupied the handsome house in Clyde Street, not far from the jail, which had been the residence of the well-known city magnate, Robert Dreghorn, Esq., Laird of Ruchill, near to Maryhill and Possil, an estate recently purchased by the Corporation of Glasgow for a public park.

The house referred to had the reputation of being *haunted;* and in addition thereto, the mob had become possessed with the idea that its then occupant, Mr. Provand, a bold, tall, and vigorous man, was that obnoxious character, a resurrectionist; and it might be even worse, a burker!

As set forth in a proclamation issued by the lord provost and magistrates, the house was broken into and entered by a riotous and tumultuous assemblage of persons, who, besides breaking the windows and destroying many articles of furniture in the house, were guilty of stealing and carrying away therefrom a number of gold, silver, and copper coins, silver plate, etc. Others of them who had not an eye to plunder, indulged their propensity for devastation and destruction, furniture being smashed, burned, or carried out and thrown into the river, which flowed past quite handy for the purpose. The police of the city were overpowered, pelted with stones, and forced to run for their lives; while about four o'clock, when the worshippers in the churches were coming out, the whole city was in a ferment. The magistrates, and Mr. James Hardie, master of police, and some well-known citizens, in vain sought to throw oil on the troubled waters. They were hooted, pelted, and driven away; Mr. Lawrence Craigie, acting-chief magistrate, having a most narrow escape for his life. In these circumstances he rushed over to the Cavalry Barracks, then in Laurieston; while one or other of his colleagues ran to the Infantry Barracks, then in the Gallowgate, for military aid.

Mr. Craigie, mounted on a dragoon horse, soon appeared at full gallop over the old Jamaica Bridge, heading the cavalry, while the infantry soon also came forward in double quick order. The Riot Act was read; the dragoons charged with drawn sabres; and the infantry advanced with fixed bayonets; on which the mob, innocent and guilty, took to their heels and fled. Next morning the lord provost and magistrates offered—

" A reward of two hundred guineas "

to any persons, who, within one month, should give such information as would lead to the apprehension and conviction of the offenders.

In consequence of said proclamation and reward, various persons were apprehended, five of whom were brought to trial before the Circuit Court of Justiciary in April following. They were convicted; and one, Richard Campbell, weaver, who had been a police officer, in addition to the sentence of transportation beyond seas, which all received, was further adjudged to be scourged through the city, by the hangman, on the 8th day of May following.

Accordingly, on the day specified, at twelve o'clock a strong detachment of the 4th Dragoon Guards paraded in front of the jail; while, at the same time, a large force of police and civil officers attended. The culprit was brought out of the jail, and bound to the cart; parties of the dragoons were placed in front and rear to keep off the crowd; and when all was ready the cavalcade moved on to the respective places of punishment. The *first* halt was made on the south side of the jail; where the culprit's back was laid bare by the hangman, who there gave him his first twenty lashes with a formidable " cat o' nine tails."

This remarkable tale, reproduced from Robert Alison's The Anecdotage of Glasgow *(1892), manages to combine body-snatching, haunting, looting, a riot and the last public whipping by the last Glasgow hangman, Thomas Young. The miscreant actually received eighty lashes – twenty at the jail, a further twenty at one end of Stockwell Street, twenty more at the other end and a final twenty at Glasgow Cross. The report finishes by saying that Young was: 'the last permanent finisher of the law maintained by the magistrates of Glasgow, his house being within the jail, from which he but seldom issued forth.'*

leaving her home in Mount Vernon to attend a dance at Uddingston. Manuel stalked, raped and strangled Isabelle and then buried her body in a nearby field; he later led police to the spot.

Peter Smart (forty-five), Doris Smart (fifty-two) and Michael Smart (ten), shot at home in Uddingston on 1 January 1958. Manuel then lived in the house for a few days, and even fed the cat; it was stealing brand-new banknotes that Peter Smart had taken out for a planned family holiday that eventually gave him away, although he also took the Smarts' car – and used it to give a lift to a police officer investigating the disappearance of Isabelle Cooke.

When Manuel was tried at the High Court in Glasgow, he dismissed his legal team and conducted his own defence with what the judge, Lord Cameron, called 'a skill that is quite remarkable', but failed to convince the jury of his insanity.

AD 1843

TRANSPORT THEM!

A **VARIETY OF OFFENCES,** from theft and housebreaking to reset (receiving stolen goods) plagued Glasgow. In the nineteenth century, such offences could lead to transportation, imprisonment or execution by hanging. The range of offences is interesting, and some today would be considered quite trivial: stealing cotton smocks, for example.

Some more grisly offences occurred too. John M'Bryde, servant with John Mason, farmer at Bulloch's Mill, Rutherglen, was accused of shooting John Allan, a labourer from Havannah Street, on 23 December 1842, in a potato field near Rutherglen. He pleaded guilty to the crime of culpable homicide.

In 1843, William M'Neil was charged with cutting and stabbing with a knife a girl in Greenock. Charles M'Kay, meanwhile, was accused in the same year of the murder of his wife. On Sunday, 18 December 1812 he attacked Catherine M'Kechnie, or M'Kay, his wife, in a house in the Old Wynd, and stabbed her with a large ham knife. She died a short time afterwards, when, after the examination of a number of witnesses, he was found guilty. He was sentenced to be executed on Thursday 18 May, 'betwixt the hours of 8 and 10'.

Prisoners sentenced to be transported, meanwhile, were initially sent mainly to America, but our Colonial cousins declined to take them after the 4 July issue of the Declaration of Independence.

Fortunately, just a few years earlier, a chap called Captain Cook had bumped into Australia, which looked like it needed filling up. Transportation was actually from England, with prisoners taken, usually by sea, to be marshalled on prison hulks. These were decommissioned warships, originally used to relieve over-crowding in English prisons in the 1700s. The Industrial Revolution at the end of that century led to mass movements of people into the cities such as Glasgow, with a consequent increase in petty crime. There were more and more debtors, and towards the end of the century there were also substantial numbers of French prisoners of war.

The problem the authorities had was that there were no 'national' prisons, only local gaols. Misdemeanours could be dealt with locally and the miscreants imprisoned there, but for more severe

Scottish prisoners sentenced to transportation were first taken to London. This satirical print of 1781 by Carington Bowles shows two bearded men (meant to portray Jews), someone gnawing a bone and a small person taking snuff. This was at a time when there was no transportation to America, so the convicts were herded onto hulks in the Thames and Medway.

crimes (felonies) prisoners had to be transported to London. This was carried out by private contractors, who also had the idea of keeping the prisoners on derelict ships or 'hulks' in the Thames, in the Medway, off south-coast ports and elsewhere. There were also hulks in Bermuda. The conditions on these floating prisons were appalling, but there was no desire to go back to the old days of execution for minor crimes, so a more humane idea developed –

transport them. Some 50,000 were settled in North America – often getting land after their seven years were up – and later in Australia. The first fleet (775 prisoners) went in 1786, followed by another three large transports between 1787 and 1791.

They weren't all thieves and brigands: transportees included the Radical intellectual William Skirving, who was arrested in Scotland with three others – Thomas Muir, John Fyshe Palmer and Maurice Margarot – for writing and publishing pamphlets on parliamentary reform. They were put on prison hulks on the Thames in preparation for their journey to Australia in 1793. There is a persistent (but unreliable) story that transportees temporarily housed at Millbank prison wore jackets with POM (Prisoner of Millbank) stencilled on the back, which explains why, to this day, Britons in Australia are called 'Poms'.

There were no prison hulks in Scotland, but we can't feel smug about that as the overseer of the Thames hulks was one Duncan Campbell, son of the principal of Glasgow University, a major tobacco shipper, prisoner-transporter and slave-runner, and the man who put Captain Bligh in charge of the *Bounty* for that notorious voyage to bring breadfruit from Tahiti as cheaper food for the slaves.

Prison ships have been used since, notably for internment of Republicans during the Irish 'troubles' of 1922 and for internees during the Second World War. In 1997 the first prison ship for 200 years off mainland UK was opened off Portland, Dorset, but within ten years was due to be closed as 'unsuitable, expensive' and 'in the wrong place'. However, severe prison overcrowding meant that the idea was revived in 2006 and again in 2010. Interestingly, detaining prisoners of war on hulks was outlawed by the 1949 Geneva Convention.

Conditions on board a prison hulk.

Other earlier reasons for transportation included being a Covenanter, being a Jacobite and, after the Act of Proscription (1747), wearing the tartan. This was repealed in 1782, but for almost two generations the tartan, pipes etc were not a normal part of life in Scotland – apart from the exemption for soldiers. The repeal, issued in Gaelic and English, was as follows:

Listen Men. This is bringing before all the Sons of the Gael, the King and Parliament of Britain have forever abolished the act against the Highland Dress; which came down to the Clans from the beginning of the world to the year 1746. This must bring great joy to every Highland Heart. You are no longer bound down to the unmanly dress of the Lowlander. This is declaring to every Man, young and old, simple and gentle, that they may after this put on and wear the Truis, the Little Kilt, the Coat, and the Striped Hose, as also the Belted Plaid, without fear of the Law of the Realm or the spite of the enemies.

THE IBROX DISASTERS

THERE HAVE BEEN three major incidents leading to loss of life at Ibrox, home to Rangers FC, due to the condition of the stands and stairways.

1902

On 5 April of this year, as the British Championship match between England and Scotland was being played, the rear of the newly built West Tribune Stand collapsed. This was later blamed on unexpectedly heavy rainfall the night before. Hundreds of supporters fell as much as 40ft to the ground under that stand: twenty-five supporters died, and over 500 were injured.

The match was only just into the second half. It was therefore decided to play on so that a mass exodus of the crowd would not impede the rescue work. However, the game was declared void by the Football Associations of both countries, who agreed to a replay at Aston Villa's ground in Birmingham on 3 May. All proceeds went to the Ibrox disaster fund.

There was one positive outcome of the tragedy – the usual wooden terracing held up by steel girders was abandoned all over Britain and terracing was supported by reinforced concrete or banked-up earthworks, making spectators everywhere much safer. A prosecution of the contractor accused of causing death through negligence collapsed.

One of the starkest testimonies to the disaster came, strangely, from a foreign visitor. A young man from Hamburg sent a postcard home on April 7, two days after the disaster, which came up for auction in 2008 and was quoted by Ian Duff, author of *Follow, Follow: Classic Rangers Old Firm Clashes* and *Temple of Dreams: The Changing Face of Ibrox*.

On Saturday I went to the big football match with my landlord and doctor. I had never seen such a crowd of people. There was an accident – it was a bit horrific. First of all the people at the back pushed forwards, so that the people at the front were crushed against some railings and many fainted.

The spectator area rises very high up and is built like a staircase. It looks a bit like a spectator area in Spain for bull-fighting. You can imagine just how terrible it seemed. It was a bit like a hangar.

Shortly before the start of the football match the upper part of the terraces collapsed and a crowd of spectators fell through the construction about 50 feet high, 99 steps, each step was three inches high. So you can imagine just how high it was.

Of course then there was terrible confusion and the crowd surged forward on to the pitch, where play should have gone on, so that the game was almost totally disrupted and mounted police had to keep order. A great many were injured. To date two are dead and about 300 injured.

We were not standing far from it all. However, the people here take sport too seriously and first of all little notice was taken. One man, who had fallen 50 feet, even got up again and watched the match through to the end. But this man, although he picked himself up straightaway, seemed afterwards to be very ill. That is the last time I shall go to a football match.

1961

There had been safety concerns over the stairway next to passageway thirteen, which led to the exit nearest the underground station at Copland Road. These were justified – on 16 September 1961, two spectators were killed in a crush on the stairway. The club spent a great deal of money improving things, but this did not prevent injuries at two other incidents, in 1967 and 1969.

1971

Disaster struck again on Saturday, 2 January 1971 during an Old Firm game against Celtic with an attendance of over 80,000. In the closing minute of the game, Celtic scored the only goal of the match. Thinking it was all over, many Rangers supporters started to leave. But Rangers star Colin Stein scored an equaliser, causing some to stop. When the final whistle went, thousands were either leaving the stadium by the infamous stairway thirteen, or trying to. Someone fell – perhaps a child carried on an adult's shoulders – and there was a huge pile-up,

The statue at the stadium.

causing a stack of bodies up to 6ft deep. Sixty-six fans were killed, mostly by suffocation, and more than two hundred others were injured.

Speculation – fuelled by certain tabloid newspapers – that the fans who had left the ground early when Celtic scored had tried to turn back was scotched by the official inquiry into the tragedy. But it still led the then-manager of Rangers, Willie Waddell, to drive a major redevelopment of Ibrox over three years, culminating in 75 per cent all-seater stands, a further conversion to a capacity of 44,000 in 1981 and even more reconstruction in the 1990s, which increased this to 50,000 and UEFA five-star status.

In 2001, the thirtieth anniversary of the disaster, a monument was unveiled which commemorated the fans who died, with blue plaques bearing their names and a statue of John Greig, captain at the time. But it was Willie Waddell who summed it up with his memory of the fatal day in 1971:

It's strange what comes into your mind, but when I first went to the top of the steps and looked down on the pile of bodies, my initial thought was of Belsen, because the corpses were entangled as they had been in the pictures which came out of the concentration camps but, my God, it was hellish, there were bodies in the dressing rooms, in the gymnasium, and even in the laundry room. My own training staff and the Celtic training staff were working at the job of resuscitation, and we were all trying everything possible to bring breath back to those crushed limbs.

There has been a recent disaster at Ibrox: the collapse, in 2012, not just of the stands but of the club itself, in a cloud of accusations over financial impropriety. For those who think football is a matter of life and death, recall the words of Bill Skankly, OBE: 'It's much, much more important than that.'

AD 1919

THE BATTLE OF GEORGE SQUARE

ONE OF THE most extreme riots in the history of Glasgow occurred on Friday, 31 January 1919, the day now known as 'Bloody Friday' or 'Black Friday'.

It started as a campaign for a working week shorter than the standard pre-war fifty-four hours, and the newly-negotiated forty-seven hours for the shipbuilding and engineering industries. Most egregious of all, the workers felt, was the removal of the traditional morning tea-break. There had been widespread industrial action, including the 'Forty Hours' strike'. The Glasgow Police clashed with protesters, and the government – fearing a Bolshevik uprising like those in Russia the year before – sent in the tanks to the city to prevent any further gatherings. The intention was sensible: war contracts were finishing, tens of thousands of ex-servicemen were coming home and looking for jobs, and unemployment was rising.

Over 3,000 workers met at the St Andrew's Halls on Monday 27 January, and some 40,000 Glasgow workers went on strike the same day, the number swelling to 60,000 or more according to some sources. This was Scotland's first mass picket since the Radical Rising of 1820. A mass meeting was held in George Square on the Friday to hear Glasgow Trades' Council president Manny Shinwell, and the lord provost issued the British government's response to the unions' request for intercession in the dispute.

The situation was not helped by Glasgow's decision to keep the trams running while the mass protest was gathering, and fighting broke out between the police and protesters. Shinwell and others tried to quell the riot but were arrested for 'instigating and inciting large crowds of persons to form part of a riotous mob', while Sheriff MacKenzie tried to read the Riot Act – unsuccessfully, as the crowd tore it from him.

The crowd reacted to police baton charges by pulling up iron railings and using bottles from a passing lorry as projectiles. The crowd eventually headed for Glasgow Green, where again the police failed to disband them. There was fighting well into the night across the city and Lloyd George's coalition government decided military intervention was the only answer. As many as 10,000 troops arrived, with tanks, Lewis machine guns

Bloody Friday.

Soldiers were billeted in various places, including here, dossing down in front of a rather appropriate set of images, the plan for a window depicting the defence of the cathedral by the Incorporated Trades in 1579.

Manny Shinwell, Independent Labour Party activist and chairman of the Glasgow Trades' Council, and Harry Hopkins, leader of an engineering union, addressing the crowd from the front of Glasgow City Chambers.

and even a 4.5-inch howitzer to defend the City Chambers. The cattle market became a tank depot, and the North British Hotel and post office became machine-gun emplacements. It is noticeable, though, that no Scottish troops were deployed, even though there was a full battalion at Maryhill barracks – it was felt their sympathies would be with the locals.

In the aftermath, Shinwell and others were jailed and the forty-seven-hour week was agreed. Shinwell became a much-respected MP and one of the icons of the Labour Left, and, along with twenty-eight other Labour MPs elected in Scotland in the 1922 General Election, took part in the first Labour government led by Ramsay MacDonald a year later. Red Clydeside had arrived!

This is said to have been the last reading in mainland Britain of the Riot Act, which was not repealed until 1973.

AD 1920-1939

NO MEAN CITY

IN 1935 AN unemployed man and a journalist sat down to tell the story of life in their home, Gorbals. The resulting book by Alexander McArthur and H. Kingsley Long was titled *No Mean City: A Story of the Glasgow Slums*, although the last part is often missed out. It painted an unvarnished picture of the 1920s run-down housing, overcrowding in almost a third of households, deprivation, hard men, razor gangs and open warfare for territory – but also the fierce pride and determination of the working class. The title comes from Paul the Apostle, who says he hails from Tarsus, which is 'no mean city'.

Much hated by the Glasgow elite, the novel – albeit a work of fiction – was widely applauded as the authoritative account of life in the Southside, and its title became a byword for the whole of Glasgow. The locals still use it as a badge of honour today. The book has sold more than 500,000 copies worldwide and has never gone out of print.

It didn't get such a good reception from the *Glasgow Evening Times* when it first appeared: the paper accused McArthur and Long of giving the city an image that was all 'thugs and harlots' and said, with its High Dudgeon turned up to eleven:

> One cannot quite swallow all the ferocity and venomous hatred, the idolatry of the Razor King, the lust and the entire absence of any code of moral behaviour... The book is undoubtedly the worst possible advertisement Glasgow can have at a time when the city is striving to live down its evil and undeserved reputation abroad.

Alexander McArthur never managed to follow the success of this book, and took to alcohol, finishing his life in what might be thought a suitable manner – on 4 September 1947 he went on a drinking binge, before swallowing a bottle of disinfectant and throwing himself into the Clyde.

The Glasgow razor boys were the most feared street gangs in Scotland and the UK, and Glasgow had the highest number of these – some estimates say five or six times as many as London, which had a population ten times the size of Glasgow at that time. The gangs were predominantly area-based, as their names show – the Calton Entry, the South Side Stickers and

Billy Fullerton, a leader, but not founder, of the Billy Boys – the arch-Protestant, anti-Catholic 'razor gang' of the 1920s and 1930s – probably never fought with a razor, preferring knives and bottles. His Brigton (Bridgeton) gang left as one of its legacies this rabidly sectarian chant, usually sung to the tune of 'Marching Through Georgia', itself composed to celebrate another kind of slaughter a few thousand miles away:

Hullo, Hullo / We are the Billy Boys / Hullo, Hullo/ You'll know us by our noise / We're up to our knees in Fenian blood / Surrender or you'll die / For we are / The Brigton Billy Boys.

the Beehive Boys (named for a shop at the corner of Cumberland Street and Thistle Street) – but there was also a sectarian element, as the Bridgeton Billy Boys were Protestant and the Norman Conks were Catholic. This may well have reflected the predominant populations on their home turf, as co-religionists tended to band together into what were effectively ghettos. The Bridgeton Billy Boys, who dominated the west of the Gorbals, were named partly for their founder, Billy Fullerton, who had strong Fascist leanings, and they took a leaf out of the Orange Order's book by forming bands, marching and dressing up

in a military style. They often clashed with the Norman Conks, whose territory started a mere 500 yards to the east of Bridgeton Cross. Fullerton later started a Glasgow chapter of the Ku Klux Klan and was in the British Union of Fascists, which speaks volumes for his state of mind.

By the time the war started in 1939 other groups had sprung up, including the San Toi, the Fleet, the Govan Team and, most infamous of all, the Tongs, whose name still ends up spray-painted on walls all over the city, usually followed by the untranslatable exclamation 'Ya Bass'.

The classic razor wound was to slice the cheek open from the mouth, known as a 'Glasgow Grin'.

The end of the razor gangs' reign of terror had a lot to do with the outbreak of war, when young unemployed men found another outlet for their hostilities. Credit also has to go to Sir Percy Sillitoe, chief constable of Glasgow, who had learned a thing or two about them in his earlier career with Sheffield Police. (Sillitoe also introduced the now-worldwide 'checky bunnet' for policemen, in order to make them more identifiable from everyone else who wore caps – including milkmen, gas-meter readers and cinema commissionaires.)

One of the most infamous razor-gang hard men was Patrick Carraher, 'The Fiend of the Gorbals'. In and out of prison for drink-fuelled fighting and knife crime, Carraher should have been put away for good, but wasn't. On one occasion he had been brushed off by a girl he had gone out with. Later that night, Carraher, completely drunk, saw her with her new beau, window cleaner James Durie. Durie refused Carraher's invitation to fight, despite a torrent of abuse. Durie's elder brothers heard about this clash and decided to confront Carraher, but despite being outnumbered Carraher refused to

South down the High Street in 2012 to Glasgow Cross – now considered less a historic monument than an impediment to traffic.

settle things. Instead, he shouted insults at the Durie brothers and their friends as they walked off. James Shaw, a soldier on leave who was just passing and had nothing to do with the fracas, told Carraher to shut up and behave. It was an intervention which was to have tragic consequences: when one of the Durie party turned around, they saw that Shaw was on the ground. He had been stabbed in the neck. The police arrested Carraher. Even though he had boasted about the murder, a clever defence lawyer at the Glasgow High Court trial convinced the jury that, as no one had actually seen the incident, Carraher could not be blamed. He was therefore found guilty not of murder but of the lesser charge of culpable homicide. He got a mere three years rather than the gallows.

Carraher capped off his career in November 1945 when he murdered a soldier, John Gordon, over a family feud. He stabbed a 'chib' (a sharpened chisel) into Gordon's neck. Even his own girl-friend and her brother gave evidence against him, and the jury took a scant twenty minutes to find Carraher guilty. He was hanged at Barlinnie on 6 April 1946, aged thirty-nine.

Glasgow's reputation for fighting men hadn't disappeared by the 1970s, when Frankie Miller's iconic shout 'McCafferty – yer tea's oot' was the catchphrase of the next decade after the 1979 'play for today', *Just a Boy's Game*, written by Peter McDougall, was shown on television. (Actually, it was set and filmed around Greenock and Port Glasgow, but never mind.)

AD 1941

THE CLYDEBANK BLITZ

LOOK UP THE seven-volume work *Civilian War Dead Rolls of Honour, 1939-1945*, published by the Imperial War Graves Commission. Of the almost 67,000 fatalities listed, Scotland occupies a thankfully brief section at the end of the final book. However, the majority of those fallen came from Clydebank.

On 13 and 14 March 1941, two Luftwaffe raids on the shipbuilding and armaments town killed over 500 people, and the list of names and places shows entire families and whole streets wiped out.

The first raid lasted over six hours. It was probably aimed directly at the industrial areas and shipyards, but nearby houses were extensively damaged. The second was, no question, a civilian attack intended to cow Scotland into submission and blunt morale for the war effort. It had exactly the opposite effect.

Overall, 528 people died, a further 617 were seriously wounded, and many hundreds more injured. Only seven (yes, seven) houses out of some 12,000 in the area were not damaged, and 4,000 were utterly destroyed. More than 48,000 'Bankies' were rendered homeless. Another 800 people died in surrounding areas.

In the event, the Blitz was a failure, as the main targets – John Brown's shipyard, Beardmore's factory, another ex-Beardmore plant (by then ROF Dalmuir), and the Singer works – did not sustain any real damage. The Strathclyde Hosiery Co., however, was completely demolished. Over 1,000 bombs were dropped from 460 aircraft over the two nights, but the RAF shot down only two bombers and the anti-aircraft guns none.

The British Government, fearing adverse publicity, and that if the German High Command knew they had missed their targets they might return, deliberately suppressed the news and the casualty figures, until forced to release them by local MPs. After the war, a government statement said: 'It is agreed by all observers that the bearing of the people in Clydebank was beyond praise'.

There are two war memorials in the now-rebuilt Clydebank – one opposite the Town Hall (which has a shrine to the fallen) and another on Graham Avenue – plus a special memorial to the crew of the *Piorun*, a Polish destroyer which helped defend the docks' shipyard. The names of the 528 dead are on a bronze plaque at the Blitz Memorial Old Dalnottar Cemetery (where unclaimed dead were interred), unveiled on 14 March 2009.

Writing these words exactly seventy years to the day of the raids, it's clear that the two raids are still fresh in the personal and collective memories of the folks of Clydebank. They won't forget, and neither should anyone else.

Clydebank after the Blitz, including the Singer Factory in ruins (above).

If you enjoyed this book, you may also be interested in...

Not a Guide to Glasgow
BRUCE DURIE

From western backwater to Scotland's largest and most stylish city, Glasgow has come a long way. This engaging little book is packed full of insider knowledge, facts, figures and the secrets of a city which boasts more comedians than Liverpool, more engineers than Birmingham, better education than Oxford and fabulous Victorian and Georgian architecture. Glasgow – ye cannee whack it!

978 0 7524 6634 7

Paranormal Glasgow
GEOFF HOLDER

Paranormal Glasgow digs into the strange and peculiar stories of Scotland's greatest city. With historical hauntings, UFO and big-cat sightings, time slips, spontaneous human combustion, bizarre beliefs and urban legends. There is an expose of the city's witchcraft trials, the story of the 'Gorbals vampire' of 1954, which saw hundreds of schoolchildren hunting for 'a monster with iron teeth', and the case of John Scott the Glasgow Fasting Man who allegedly survived without food or water for 106 days – and was proved to have done so by the Vatican.

978 0 7524 5420 7

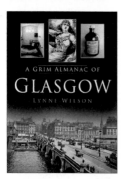

A Grim Almanac of Glasgow
LYNNE WILSON

A Grim Almanac of Glasgow is a day-by-day catalogue of 366 ghastly tales from around the city. Full of dreadful deeds, strange disappearances and a multitude of mysteries this almanac explores the darker side of Glasgow's past. Here are stories of tragedy torment and the truly unfortunate with diverse tales of brutal murders, tragic suicides and macabre events, including the experiments of Dr Andrew Ure, who, in 1818 applied electricity to the dead body of an executed murderer, animating the corpse.

978 0 7524 6194 6

The Guide to Mysterious Glasgow
GEOFF HOLDER

This is the essential guide to everything strange, marvellous, mysterious and paranormal in Glasgow, with a street-by-street description of all things bizarre and supernatural connected with the city. As well as a complete guide to all of the city's gargoyles legends and relics, it includes tours of the Necropolis, the cathedral, museums both famous and little-known, and Glasgow's hidden archaeological wonders. Insightful and entertaining, it will transform the way you experience the city.

978 0 7524 4826 8

Visit our website and discover thousands of other History Press books.

www.thehistorypress.co.uk

The History Press